The Millennium Agenda

The Goals and Deceptions of the New Age Movement in the 21st Century

Cleff Publishing
Flower Mound, Texas

Published by Cleff Publishing
P.O. Box 270014
Flower Mound, TX 75027
Copyright ©1999 by Jeff Justus
All Rights Reserved
Printed and Bound in the United States of America

Library of Congress Catalog Number: 99-97821
ISBN 0-9676350-0-4

To My Dad:

A man constantly sowing
in his own special way;
he didn't get to see
the full harvest
of his labor.

Contents

Foreword 6

Introduction 7

Section I Understanding New Age Influences .. 17

Chapter 1: A Background in World Religion 18

Chapter 2: The Roots of the New Age 27

Chapter 3: Some New Age Philosophies.................... 36

Chapter 4: Evolution 42

Chapter 5: Evolution II 49

Section II Common New Age Manifestations 55

Chapter 6: Angel Contact 56

Chapter 7: Alien Contact 61

Chapter 8: Witches, Crystals, and Candles 75

Chapter 9: Near Death Experiences and
    Afterlife Contact 83

**Section III False Prophets and The Fading
    Christ** 93

Chapter 10: Doubting Thomas 94

Chapter 11: Priestess of Isis 110

Chapter 12: Would the "Real" Christ Please
    Stand Up 125

Chapter 13: Secret Societies and the
    Priori de Sion 137

Chapter 14: Is it Christian or Not? 150

**Section IV Current Events and End-Time
    Prophecy** 173

Chapter 15: The One-World Government 174

Chapter 16: The Next Stage................................ 181

Glossary 192

Index 195

Foreword

At the dawn of the new millennium, there are many beacons sending out messages but there is only one that is truly good news. In this book, my friend Jeff Justus shines forth the bright light of the message of the good news of Jesus Christ.

If you are trying to make sense of schoolyard killings, war, broken families, alienated communities, and empty lives, Jeff has given you a way to identify the lies and find the truth. Jesus Christ said, "You will know the truth, and the truth will set you free." Take the truth of this book, live by its principles, and find abundant life in the here and the hereafter.

Dr. Ben Smith, Pastor
Lakeland Baptist Church
Lewisville, Texas

Introduction

The Millennium Agenda

About this Book

This book is not intended to tell you what to do or what not to do. This book is intended to make the average person aware of the vast spectrum of New Age influences that surround us all. In many cases, people unwittingly have become involved in or have absorbed some form of New Age philosophy. The primary reason for this is the subtle nature in which it is conveyed. In fact, the New Age philosophy can be carried in things so innocuous as a toothpaste commercial.

As Christians, we have the responsibility to know what we are dealing with. Just as you read the label of your food products we are to scrutinize the contents of activities in which we engage for growth and entertainment. I hope you will find this study enlightening and that it will help you screen New Age influences for you and your family. What you do with this information, whether you begin or quit certain activities, is entirely up to you and should be governed by your religious convictions.

In business, executives will look at many factors in order to judge what will be the future trends. In particular, history tends to be a good predictor of what will come, given similar circumstances, driving factors, and desired outcomes.

I find this also to be true of the New Age. I believe that the New Age, or rather the forces behind the New Age, are subject to the same driving factors and desired outcomes that have existed for ages. What we will see in this book is that the circumstances are being prepared for a devastating battle.

How Long Has This Been Going On?

The "New Age" has been flourishing around us for the last few years. It sounds like something new, but the movement has been in the works since Adam and Eve were expelled from the Garden of Eden. When one considers the history of the movement, it is difficult to keep from becoming overwhelmed by its size and momentum. I believe the New Age movement is the capstone of Satan's plot to enslave the world.

The term "New Age" is, in fact, a fairly recent term, but the movement has also been called the "New World Order," "The Third Wave," "The Aryan Age," and many other less common names.

The term "New Age" was developed over two decades ago, but has become popularized by its identity with the new millennium, New Age music, and other benign things.

The New Age religion does not classify **sin** as an absolute. In fact, sin, and **morals** in general, are situational and relative. This being the case, there need not be accountability for sin since there is no absolute authority. One needs only to justify his sins against the situation and the offended. For example, if a homeless person steals an apple, it's okay because he did not possess the means to buy it.

New Agers, then, consider the **Bible** to consist of fables and legend, none of which constitute a moral absolute by which to govern their lives. This philosophy holds for the New Testament as well. This means that they believe that **Jesus** was a man, perhaps even a prophet, who had reached Nirvana. They believe that He was not God the Creator, nor did He carry our sin debt to the cross.

And since Jesus was only a mere mortal who was able to reach Nirvana, then **"Christ"** takes on an entirely different meaning. Many New Agers believe "Christ" to be a state of being; that is, the whole of society being of one consciousness. Others believe Christ to be the One who will rule the world—but not Jesus the man.

"God," they believe, is everything. Or, in some cases, nothing. This is a confusing concept for Christians to grasp because the New Age phrases are so similar to Christian terminology that the differences are often overlooked. For example, the term "godhead" is used by Krishnas, but has nothing to do with the Christian God. To New Agers, god is not a personality as much as it is a state of being. This "state of being" is that in which the physical world exists in a utopian condition and life transcends the physical realm: Nirvana. A good example of this is found in the Star Trek series when a "life form" is encountered which is "pure energy." To many, **nature** itself is the embodiment of god. One uniform concept, however, is that "god" is impersonal.

New Agers **pray**, but to whom do they pray? They pray to nature, and they seek to evoke the energy, also called the Life Force, of the universe. The specific form of prayer, **meditation**, entreats the person to clear his or her mind of all previous notions of good and evil so that they can receive the "enlightened" view of the universe and life.

Evangelism is very unpopular. The reason, as New Agers believe, is that all religions lead to God. The concept of diversity means that we all accept each other's religion without bias, since whichever religion a person chooses is the appropriate religion for him or her. In other words, **religion** is merely a noble exercise in discipline, but has nothing necessarily to do with the eternal fate of the soul. **Angels** are simply the kind helpers who guide us and help us evolve to our next state, the state of being a god. And **Christianity** in its current form will become a fatal endeavor. Christians will ultimately stand against the New Age movement and this will be perceived as a traitorous act.

What Have UFOs Got To Do With the New Age?

They are demonic. There is no evidence to support the idea of life on other planets. In fact, the odds are greatly against life on other planets. The "aliens," however, seem bent on passing on New Age philosophy. They even drop the name of Jesus occasionally.

Dr. Hugh Ross, an astrophysicist and president of Reasons To Believe, says that over two dozen parameters must be just right in order for life on any planet to be possible.[1] If any one of the parameters is too great or too small, then the whole formula is inviable. (See Chapter 7.)

Angels in the New Age

Angels have become a popular New Age item. Many people claim to have guardian angels with which they converse on a regular basis. The New Age angels are, more than likely, agents of Satan masquerading as holy angels in an effort to deceive those unaware of the danger.

New Age angels have commonly given history, prophecy, and doctrine to their human contacts. Those messages have turned out to be occult (and sometimes overtly satanic) in nature.

The angels of the Bible were created specifically for the purpose of delivering messages from God and serving God. Their appearances are rare and brief. See Chapter 6.

Why Can't I Watch Cartoons Anymore?

Are you kidding? Have you actually watched them lately? They are fraught with pagan and occult doctrine. Case in point: Do you remember the phrase "by the power of Greyskull?"

Contemporary cartoons teach kids how to pray to Satan and conjure up spirits. Kids learn that they are reincarnated, that they can be telepathic, and that they can have telekinetic power. They learn also that one need only be a good person to be accepted by god (little "g" on purpose).

It's Just a Game!

Computer games have set the pace in desensitizing kids and adults alike in such matters as killing another human. Games like *Mortal Kombat, DOOM* and others feature combat situations in which the player must kill the opponent(s). Peter and Paul Lalonde, coauthors of *2000 A.D. Are You Ready?* made the following observation.

> **In one game, Rise of the Triad, Nazi soldiers
> are the enemy, and to win the game, you
> have to kill them all. Often, during the
> course of the game, you may wound a soldier
> but not actually kill him. The wounded man**

> **falls to his knees and waves his hands in the
> air saying "No, please, don't shoot, please,
> please don't shoot." If you don't shoot him,
> however, he will pull out a gun and *shoot
> you*. In other words, if you don't kill this
> guy, with his hands in the air, begging for
> his life, then you will lose the game![2]**

In the game *DOOM*, the player must work his way through a
maze and shoot every living creature. As he progresses, the
imagery encountered is more and more satanic; images such as
inverted pentagrams (upside-down star which is almost always
considered satanic), devilish looking skulls, and goat heads. At
the advanced levels of the maze, the user is subjected to images of
human mutilation. At one point, the player encounters an image
of a decapitated human head on a stake. I have heard rumors
that this was the image of the author of the game.

Other features of the game include a "god" mode in which the
player becomes immortal.

Games like *Diablo* and *Dungeons and Dragons* feature situations
where the player progresses through the game by use of magic.
The player can become more and more powerful as he (his
character, that is) learns more spells. The player will find these
spells in books or scrolls that he acquires in the course of the
game. He can also learn spells from other players in the game.
These games also feature unbridled killing. In *Dungeons and
Dragons* the player can choose the characteristics of his game-
piece. Evil characters inherently are more powerful and more
likely to win the game.

These are just a few examples, but the effect is what is most
disturbing. Even if your kids don't go out and shoot anybody,
their general regard for human life may be severely altered—not
to mention that they will have been thoroughly introduced to
occult, and often Satanic, symbolism.

What About People Who Have Died, Visited Heaven (or Hell) and Come Back to Life?

This is called a Near Death Experience (NDE). It is considered "near" because it is not final.

Not all of the persons who have been clinically dead (loss of vital signs) and been resuscitated claim to have had NDEs.

However, of those who do experience a NDE, the great majority find the experience to be life changing. And, the overwhelming messages they bring from the experience are New Age in nature. (See Chapter 9.)

Didn't Jesus Claim To Be the "Light"? If So, Then Why Is the New Age Concept of Light Considered To Be Bad?

True, Jesus is the "light of the world," but Satan is the great deceiver and will put on any disguise to mislead the casual Christian.

> **And I will keep on doing what I am doing in order to cut the ground from under those who want an opportunity to be considered equal with us in the things they boast about. For such men are false apostles, deceitful workmen, masquerading as apostles of Christ. And no wonder, *for Satan himself masquerades as an angel of light* (II Corinthians 11:12 - 14 NIV).**

It is important to test all angels, prophets, and spirits.

The New Age Has So Many Good Parts, How Can It Be So Bad?

Have you ever heard of a "rider"? That's when congress includes a particularly unpleasant issue at the end of a very attractive bill. The bill will pass for its positive value in spite of its negative aspects.

The Millennium Agenda

Satan wants to sell the New Age philosophy as such a good thing that everyone, including Christians, will be misled into following it. By embedding a lie in so much "goodness," people often buy into the lie without realizing it.

Is Hollywood Involved?

This would appear to be the case. Almost every movie produced in the United States for the last forty years (more increasingly in the later years) has some manifestation of New Age philosophy. However, rather than being a global plot, I believe the movie producers are merely willing but unwitting pawns of Satan's plan.

In the last ten years, one would be hard-pressed to find a movie that did *not* have some New Age bias.

The popular TV show, Dharma and Greg features a young couple and the wife practices yoga and spouts New Age jargon. Dharma, by the way is a Hindu term refering to the Hindu moral code. The term is also used in Buddhism and Jainism.

What Does the New Age Philosophy Teach?

The essential message of the New Age movement is based on evolution. According to New Age teaching, over millions or billions of years (depending on whom you ask) man has reached the Aquarian age and is on the brink of the Aryan age. However, mankind cannot move into the Aryan age until all elements of society are in place.

Those elements are a one-world government, the establishment of a one-world religion, a unified consciousness among all humankind, and a oneness with god (little "g" intentional). The term "unified consciousness" specifically refers to meditation. Meditation is, in some cases, considered prayer, but is not like prayer in the sense that one is talking to God. Meditation is a practice of focusing one's thoughts, typically on self-improvement, self-evolution, or some occult subject. True prayer is communication and petition with the almighty, personal God.

Beware of courses like **Silva Mind Control,**[3] which claim to be the "next phase of human evolution on this planet." They are designed to help people develop psychic abilities. **Visualization** is the use of mental concentration and directed mental imagery in the attempt to secure particular goals, whether physical, psychological, vocational, or spiritual.

Examples

Yin Yang is an Oriental symbol that represents the Eastern religious concept of good and evil. The concept is that good and evil *must* coexist. Good cannot exist without the conflict imposed by evil. Evil would not be evil if it were not for the presence of good. It is the constant interaction of these two which causes all things to be. In the essence of good is the potential for evil and in the essence of evil is the potential for good. This symbol is usually visible at martial arts studios and presentations.

An advertisement from a novelty catalog I came across claimed that an amulet could prevent illness. The ad claims that the device was "developed by a doctor" and "contains a series of crystals that vibrate at frequencies helping pace your natural energy shield." It also says that the device is "in tune" with your "biokenetic energy." Energy and crystals both play a major role in New Age philosophy.

Biokenetic energy is a purely New Age concept. It has no scientific basis.

A direct-mail advertisement distributed by Microsoft a few years ago features a handful of tarot cards amidst several other mystic-looking devices. This advertisement was for a software package. Tarot cards are used for fortune telling which is also an integral part of the New Age movement. This type of advertising demonstrates that the marketing executives at Microsoft find tarot (fortune telling) cards so commonplace that they do not fear insulting any major segment of the population.

The Millennium Agenda

I recently saw a book titled *ANGEL POWER and How to Use It* for sale in a 1950s era novelty catalog. This book had nothing in common with the other products in the catalog. It is apparent the editors of this catalog are selling more than just 1950s novelties.

Don't forget the original book on Angel Power, the Bible.

Section I

Understanding New Age Influences

The Millennium Agenda

Chapter 1: A Background in World Religion

Let's start by exploring some religious concepts. **Monotheism** is the idea of an exclusive single God as in Judaism, Christianity, and Islam. These three stand alone in this idea.

Monism advocates that all things, both material and spiritual, are conceived as a unified whole. There is no ultimate distinction between things. One could say, for instance, that the spirit of his or her cat is one and the same with that of a tree.

Pantheism identifies everything with god and god with everything. Everything *is* god. Similar to monism, pantheism raises all matter to deity. Impersonal, but godly.

Gnosticism is a cult that developed in the period of the early Church. Gnosticism implies that salvation comes through knowledge rather than faith. People who claim to be Christian Gnostics state that salvation is a product of the knowledge of (or relationship with) God rather than of works or faith. But, the root of gnosticism is more radical than this. It generally is stated that knowledge of God is one's salvation, that knowledge supersedes faith, and that faith alone is futile.

Polytheism is most commonly recognized as the myths and legends of Rome, Greece, and Egypt. In polytheism, there are many gods making up a society of gods of varying authority and power. There is no explanation of the origin of the gods or from where they derive their power (since it varies from one to the next).

Animism is characterized by spirits that are concerned with human affairs and are capable of helping or harming human interests. These spirits communicate, materialize, and otherwise interact with humans. The movie *Ghost* with Demi Moore and Patrick Swayze is a good example of animism.

Energy is a New Age philosophy in which all things are a translation of energy and humans can control that energy. Ironically, this is linked to Einstein's equation: $E=MC^2$. The theory states that energy and matter are essentially the same, and that one can be converted into the other. Einstein's theory was a postulation on physics, not a metaphysical statement.

Hinduism

Hindus claim that Hinduism is the oldest religion, having begun about 1500 B.C. in India. This is about the same time as the tower of Babel (using King James dating). It was originally very ritualistic. The rituals became so complicated that the people had to go through the priests to perform the rites of purification.

This allowed the priests to gain great power since they were the mediators to the gods. The people revolted in about 600 B.C. and Jainism, a new form of the religion. resulted which was less ritualistic.

In Hinduism, god, or Brahman, is impersonal. People are merely extensions of Brahman, as it were, a dream of Brahman. Hinduism espouses the ideas of Karma and Reincarnation, and the goal is Liberation.

The words **Karma** and **Reincarnation** necessarily go together. Karma is deeds or works, and the class into which one is reincarnated is based on those deeds or Karma in the past (or current) life. **Liberation** or salvation is when the individual realizes that his individuality is a mere illusion and the goal is to assimilate into the nothingness of Brahman.

By the way, you may have seen pictures or posters that are composed in Indian style with a central male figure with a light blue skin tone. This figure is Krishna and is the seventh reincarnation of Vishnu. Vishnu is one of the principal Hindu deities and is worshiped as the protector and preserver of worlds. Krishna is revered as a figure who has reached liberation or Nirvana.

Jainism

Jainism is the variant form of Hinduism resulting from the revolt that occurred in about 600 B.C. This form of Hinduism does not

The Millennium Agenda

teach that there is a creator and espouses the doctrine of ahimsa, which prohibits injury to any living creature.

Buddhism

Buddhism developed about 600 B.C. in a part of India which is now Nepal. This would be about the time that the Jews were captive in Babylon. Siddartha Gautama, the founder of Buddhism, was born into a wealthy family. He mused about the suffering of life (I can hardly imagine that he really suffered in his wealth).

Siddartha Gautama concluded that life is suffering and that to live is to suffer. Further, everything is temporal and all things will pass. The way to eliminate suffering, he determined, was to eliminate desire: If you want for nothing, then you will have need for nothing.

The way to eliminate desire was through ethical conduct, attaining wisdom, and mental discipline. And the goal, like Hinduism, is Nirvana. But, unlike Hinduism, in Buddhism the same individual (personality) does not reincarnate. According to Buddha, the individual is made up of five parts that come together at birth and dissipate at the time of death and thus the identity of the individual ceases to exist. The five parts remain, but since they are no longer related, then they no longer form the identity.

Siddartha Gautama was considered the first Buddha and is revered as a prophet.

Taoism

Taoism developed in China circa 1100 B.C. and is also called Ritual Music.

All culture was guided by rituals; i.e., how to relate to others, how to conduct business, etc. It was called "Music" since the rituals were to be executed with artistic exactness.

The main tenets include the **Tao** which is the indescribable, that is, heaven. There really are no gods, but a heaven which transends understanding. The *Te* is the individual's connection to the universal Tao. The concept of **Inactivity** is "letting nature take its course" versus imposing force. If someone steals your crops, then do nothing to retaliate. To retaliate is to create even further strife. This is not to say that Taoism condones theft. The objective of Taoism is peace in one's life. This is achieved mainly by not allowing one's self to become agitated by events that may or may not be in his or her control.

Yin Yang is the concept of the opposing but balancing forces of nature. In a classical sense, evil versus good: Good cannot be defined were it not for the existence of evil, or darkness could not be defined were it not for the existence of light. This concept states that both opposites must exist. If either overcomes the other, then the opposition, and all existence, will cease. Think of it this way: In order for a magnet to work, there must be a positive and a negative pole. These forces are equal, and opposite. If, however, a magnet loses its charge (both poles become positive or negative) then it ceases to be a magnet. This is how Taoism sees all forces of nature.

Confucianism

Confucianism was developed in China circa 500 B.C. Taoism had collapsed and Confucius wanted to restore the Ritual Music society but was unable to do so.

Confucius questioned the concept of moral absolutes. In the absence of some moral standard, all morals became relative. Society, then, dictated morality.

He believed in the concept of the "JEN" (ideal humanity) and that all people were innately good. It was that goodness, he believed, that could sustain the society.

The Millennium Agenda

Shinto

Developed in Japan, this religion predates any record. It emphasizes community over individuality (case in point: kamikaze pilots). It incorporates the idea of indebtedness. For instance, if I give you a gift, you then are indebted to me. This is most popularly known as the idea that saving one's life makes that person indebted to you.

There are many gods (who procreate other gods). The gods indwell material objects and may be good or evil at will. The gods are only for Japan. The Shinto can attain purity with the gods through their own efforts.

The goal of Shinto is to reach a state of a superior man or intellectual Gentry. Or, in other words, when the individual is actualized by his full potential and has reached moral perfection. This is achieved by the practice of self-reflection, self-cultivation,

Religion	God	Personality of God
Animism	Beyond our abilities to know or communicate with.	Undefined
Buddhism	Nirvana; an abstract void	None
Confucianism	General; Heaven	None
Hinduism	Impersonal	None
Islam	Singular	Personal
Shinto	Many gods	Kind or evil at will
Tao	A force	Impersonal
Christianity	Singular; triune	Kind; loving

and moral responsibility. This is only possible in Shinto because the true nature of mankind is goodness.

Islam

Developed in Arabia around 600 A.D., Islam advocates that god is singular and autonomous and to associate another with him as equal is heresy. In other words, the idea of the Trinity is heresy. Islam has angels in several ranks from Gabriel the archangel to Jinn (from which we get the word genie), the lowest angel.

Their holy book is the Qur'an (pronounced Kor-**an**).

Moslems (adherants of Islam) believe that they will ultimately be judged by their deeds, not by faith.

They have a common heritage with the Jews since they, too, claim

Focus	Objective	Method
Spirits	Deals only with immediate issues	Via spirits
Eliminate suffering	Eliminate desires; Nirvana	Self reliance and discipline
Man's innate goodness	Moral order	Education; self-reflection
Liberation from illusion and ignorance	Merge into oneness and the individual disappears	Self discipline
Man's goodness	More good deeds than bad	Good deeds
Pleasing the gods		Purification through rituals
	Order and harmony in society	Go with the flow
Personal holiness	Kingdom of God	Salvation through faith

to be descendants of Abraham by Ishmael. This, in fact, is the root of the dissension between the Jews and the Arabs for the Holy Land of Israel.

Thought Processes

Martial Arts and Yoga

The martial arts claim to work by unifying mind, spirit, and body through meditation and physical discipline.

The problem is that people who practice a martial arts program primarily for physical fitness purposes can still be influenced by its underlying religious philosophy. Most methods of martial arts incorporate some form of Eastern philosophy and meditation.

Yoga is the practice of meditation, mind control, and body control to achieve enlightenment. It is difficult to separate the physical aspects of yoga from the spiritual aspects. Yoga utilizes Hindu philosophies.

I recently saw a local news broadcast which featured a story of a woman who uses yoga as a treatment for Attention Deficit Disorder (ADD & ADHD). According to the story, practicing yoga helps children focus on relaxing. During the few minutes that I watched the interview, I was able to identify several New Age techniques that were expressed either by the instructor or the students.

Transmission Meditation

This is a form of meditation that is described as "the simplest, most potent way to serve humanity and help transform our world."[4] The purpose of this meditation is to focus energy from some unknown source to a central repository to be used by the "masters." The masters are spirits that exist in the planetary hierarchy. New Age and Eastern religions maintain that this "hiearchy" is the structure of the spiritual world . These masters are the supposed source of spiritual teaching via telepathy, chaneling, and automatic writing.

In Transmission Meditation, members sit in a circle or horseshoe formation and recite mantras or the "Great Invocation."

The Great Invocation is a non-denominational, in fact, all-encompassing prayer, which seeks to unite all religions under one prayer. This prayer was written by Alice Bailey. (See Chapter 11 for more information on Alice Bailey.) The meditation supposedly works by focusing energy to the "masters" so it can thus be used for the betterment of society.

On the preceding pages is a comparison of the various religious structures mentioned in this chapter.

Cults and the Occult

Cults are religions that are not classified under any of the broadly defined religions that we have discussed so far. For a religion to be considered "occult" it only needs to deal in the "unknown" or mystical world.

The number of religions that fall under this category are numerous. However, in my studies, I have come across several consistencies between the teachings of various occult religions.

Emphasis on "Love"
Many Christian-like occult religions focus on love as the central, driving theme. They claim love is the answer to all of mankind's problems. They frequently make reference to Jesus' teachings of love.

Downplay of Jesus' Divinity
These religions end up trying to reduce all phenomena to natural events. In so doing, they reduce the virgin birth, miracles, and resurrection of Jesus to speculation.

Repeated Use of "Christ" Without "Jesus"
Cults do a lot of talking about Christ, but do not indicate that Jesus is *the* Christ; or, they claim that Jesus achieved Christhood from mortality. Some also claim that Jesus is merely one of many christs, and still others claim that everyone has the potential to become a christ.

The Millennium Agenda

Sketchy Authority

Occult religions proclaim their own authority, or claim to have been given the doctrine from some authority. These cults that are Christian-like usually claim that their doctrine was received from an angel, or Jesus, but end up explaining away all or part of the gospel as recorded in the Bible.

Usually in refuting their opposition, many cult religions use phrases like "nothing could be further from the truth." They offer no authority for the contradiction. One author stated it this way: "Nothing could be more erroneous than such an idea."

I have seen phrases like these many times in my study.

Appeal to Reason Versus Faith

Cults and the occult will make an appeal to reason. In other words, they argue that their religion is to be observed since it makes reasonable sense.

Christianity, on the other hand, appeals to faith. The Bible says that the wisdom of God is foolishness to man and conversely, the wisdom of man is foolishness to God.

If a religion makes reasonable sense outside of a faith experience, then it is probably not of God.

Promise of Knowledge

In the Garden of Eden, Satan promised knowledge to Eve. His persuasion was not for her to transgress on a commandment; his persuasion was that she would gain knowledge.

Many New Age and occult religions promise knowledge. They sound an awful lot like the old alchemists who tried to turn lead into gold. We now know that is not possible (at least with current and foreseeable technology). But these religions make the same kinds of claims in terms of knowledge.

Chapter 2: The Roots of the New Age

Satan Causes Man's Fall - Garden of Eden

Man was created for a specific purpose: communion with God. His secondary purpose was to have dominion over the earth. Man was also created with a free will, unlike the angels. Man could choose his destiny. By giving man free will, God also had to give him an *option*. That option was in the form of a single tree, from which man was forbidden to eat. The law and the consequences were clear: To eat from the tree was a death penalty.

Satan, in an attempt to thwart God's plan, tempts the woman to eat the fruit of the tree. His approach was not a direct affront to God's law, but rather a twist of the wording of that law. In so doing, Satan introduced confusion and doubt into Eve's mind. This was to become the method of choice for Satan and his demons.

Even though Adam and Eve ate the fruit, and their fate was sealed, God provided for a Savior even in their sentence. The Savior would come in the form of a blood sacrifice.

Satan Attempts To Corrupt Humankind

Satan, now well aware that a Savior will come from the offspring of the woman, attempts to corrupt every family on earth. Doing this would ensure that a pure bloodline would not be available for the birth of a Savior.

The sixth chapter of Genesis makes reference to the "daughters of men" and the "sons of God." These phrases confound many people since the reference is to marriage and offspring.

Many scholars now commonly believe that "daughters of men" simply means human females, while the phrase "sons of God" refers to angelic beings. Considering the passage and the context, it is clear that these angelic beings are not holy, but rather demons.

The marriage of the daughters of men to the sons of God was

The Millennium Agenda

Satan's way of attempting to corrupt every family on earth. But Noah and his family were "just" according to Genesis 6:9, thus suggesting that he and his family exclusively were not only righteous, but had avoided corruption of their bloodline. The flood, then, was the cleansing of the corrupted bloodlines on earth.

Having failed to corrupt every bloodline on earth, and so being prohibited from human [sexual] interaction after the flood, Satan and his minions had to find another way to prevent the Savior from coming to man.

Satan Tries To Crush Israel - Majority of Old Testament

With the identification of Abraham and his offspring (namely Israel) as the "chosen" people for the coming Savior, Satan thus directs his assault on the Hebrew people.

Time after time, we see instances of unwarranted aggression and oppression of the Israelites. Even so, Satan was not able to extinguish the children of Israel.

About 700 - 400 B.C., the Israelites had fallen captive or scattered so much that the Old Testament basically discontinues its record. It would appear that Satan had succeeded. It was at this time that God chose to send the Savior to the world. He chose the lowest tribe of the Israelites, and in fact, the lowest clan (Galilee) to be the blessed family for our Savior.

Satan Attempts To Kill the Christ Child

Even when Jesus was an infant, Satan knew that He was the Savior and attempted to kill Him. Herod's advisors told him that a new "king" had been born. Hearing this, Herod ordered all male infants to be killed. He was hoping to retain his throne (he died about five years later). See Matthew 2:13.

The Blessed Family fled to Egypt and was protected.

Satan Tries To Corrupt Jesus - The Temptations

Satan now directly assaults Jesus. Satan realized the humanity of Jesus and thus tried to tempt Jesus with human desires: food, kingdoms, and power. (Luke 4.)

The temptation of the food is interesting in that food is necessary for life. The issue was that Jesus was in a period of fasting—purification. The temptation to eat would have taken focus away from His purification. Furthermore, the temptation was exactly that, temptation. As in the example of Christ, we should always flee temptation even when it seems innocent.

Satan was unable to seduce Jesus to sin and thus began to work out another strategy.

Satan Attempts To Stop the Gospel - The Crucifixion of Christ

Satan is not omniscient. He does not know the future. This means that he could not have anticipated the repercussions of his next act. Satan was unable to prevent the coming of the Christ, he was unable to prevent Jesus from reaching adulthood, and he was unable to prevent Jesus' ministry. Satan now directed a frontal assault against Jesus by turning the hearts of the Jews against Him. The Church and government were already against Him, but without the support of the people, the leaders had little power.

Since Satan was able to harden the hearts of the Jews, they cried out for Jesus' death: "Crucify Him!"—a most hideous and painful, torturous death.

Jesus accepted the crown of thorns. He walked willingly to His death. He stretched out His hands to accept the nails. In so doing, He died. In so doing, He fulfilled the prophecies of the Messiah. And in so doing, He became Savior.

Satan had failed. Even at the moment when he celebrated his victory, he had failed.

The Millennium Agenda

Satan Tries To Withhold the Gospel

By killing the Christ, Satan had caused the rampant spread of the gospel message. Jesus had arisen from the dead and shown Himself to many. His resurrection meant more than simply conquering death. His resurrection meant that He had conquered sin. The gospel was more powerful now than it ever was in Jesus' earthly lifetime.

Holy men sprang up everywhere. Satan had to use a new tactic, since he could no longer stop the coming Christ, and since the gospel message was spreading across the Middle East and Asia at an incredible rate. Satan knew that he needed to stop the spread. Satan whispered to these holy men that they should cloister themselves away from the masses. He convinced many to take oaths of silence.

Historical and archaeological evidence is flooded with accounts of monasteries throughout the Middle East and Asia where these holy men would cloister. They devoted themselves to the Scripture and prayer, but rarely evangelized. This era is known as the Byzantine period in archaeological terms. An article in *Biblical Archaeology Review* explains:

Although Christian Monasticism began in Egypt, perhaps as early as the late third century, it soon spread to Palestine. A monk named

The Great Laura, perhaps the largest monastery of its type in the Judean Desert.[5]

> Hilarion, who was born in Gaza, was active as early as 308 C.E. (A.D.) and is often considered the proto-monk of Palestine and the founder of Negev monasticism.[6]

The article continues:

> In most cases the monks arrived as pilgrims, coming to pray at the holy places in Jerusalem and elsewhere. Eventually many of them went down to join one of the communities of monks in the desert.[7]

But what Satan did not realize was that the gospel is not only for the holy men, but for everyone. The simple testimony of everyday people continued to spread the gospel.

Satan Tries To Defame Christianity

Among the tactics that Satan has used are defamation tactics. There are several accounts of atrocities that were committed in the name of Christianity, including the Crusades and the Inquisitions.

Again, while these acts caused embarrassment to the Christian church as a whole, the gospel continued to grow in the lives of individuals.

> **The Crusades and Inquisitions** occurred from about 1050 to 1300. The objective of the Crusades was to bring the Holy Land under Christian rule. They left a wake of ruthless devastation. The Inquisitions were characterized by severe penalties for beliefs and activities that were considered heresy to the Christian church.

Satan Tries To Outwit the Gospel

In the late 1800s and early 1900s, the natural and physical sciences were gaining popularity among the common people. Darwin's theory of evolution was so popular because of the volumes of methodical research. Science was now moving out of the dimly lit laboratories into the spotlight. The driving idea was that everything must be proven to be considered fact. Thus, science rallied to set aside the dogma and tradition of the Christian church because it could not be "proven."

However, in their hurry to shut the door on religion, scientists forgot to mention that there are many more phenomena in science that are unexplained than there are in religion.

Satan Tries To Deny the Gospel

At the turn of the 20th century, scientific method was undergoing some change. The exhaustive work of empirical science was reaching great popularity. In empirical science, an idea or hypothesis is "proven" based on repeated observation. Popular scientists and philosophers were claiming that all "facts" should stand the test of science. In this, they justified themselves in tossing aside faith.

For so long, Christians had believed in truths that they had (either correctly or incorrectly) interpolated from the Bible. In so doing, they laid themselves open for attack from the "scientists." These Christians who held firm to prior dogma of faith (especially when that faith juxtaposed with science) became the object of public scorn.

This gave rise to such "scientific" religions as Christian Science and the Rosicrucians (see Chapter 14). And in direct contrast to each of these was the atheist movement. The atheist movement has actually been around for several hundreds (if not thousands) of years. People want to think that they are completely autonomous. This was one of Satan's more profound tactics.

The atheist philosophy seemed to work best on the persons who considered themselves educated. Intellectuals would grasp the idea and fervently argue its merit. Scholars would propagate the message with reckless disregard for Biblical truth.

In the 1950s and '60s the idea became popular with the younger generations in America. These were the students who were exploring a freedom that had never before been afforded their age group. Mass communication was common. High-speed transportation and economic advantage allowed this generation the method and means to explore "new thought." This generation (like any) was eager to disconnect from the beliefs of their parents and elders. However, in eagerness to think free from religion, these explorers fell hook, line, and sinker into Eastern religion which does not presuppose an intelligent Creator.

An example of how this is taking place is that many scholars, even those claiming to be Christian, defame Biblical history. In an article in *Biblical Archaeology Review* the authors discuss the great deal of argument over the existence of King David of Israel. They mention a claim by Philip R. Davies, author of a book entitled *In Search of "Ancient Israel,"* that:

> **Most of Israel's history prior to the Babylonian Exile, as related to the Bible is fictional, having been created during the Persian period (sixth-fourth centuries B.C.E. [B.C.]).** [8]

After Davies' book was published, an inscription was found which made reference to the House of David. This inscription is commonly known as the Tel Dan inscription.

Of particular note in the inscription is the phrase *bytdwd*. Literally, this phrase was translated as "House of David." To this point, there had been no archaeological evidence of King David of Israel. In an article by Davies in *Biblical Archaeology Review* following the discovery of the Tel Dan inscription, Davies chose not to admit that some evidence had been found to make reference to the House of David outside of the Bible itself. Rather, he even strengthened his argument that Biblical archaeologists impressed their religious views on an inscription that could not possibly refer to King David of Israel.

In a follow-up letter to the editor, a reader disputes Davies' claim:

> **The same people who cannot accept the reference to "the House of David" in the Aramaic inscriptions from the Tel Dan are energetically writing articles to explain that the word *DWD* in the Dan inscription is not "David" but the name of a hitherto unrecog-**

> nized deity called "Dod." They are finding
> the "DOD" in the Mesha text on the Moabite
> stone and in various Biblical texts mention-
> ing the "house of David" and "the tent of
> David." They deny that David is mentioned
> in any of those places.[9]

The point here is that some scholars are spending considerable time trying to explain why certain evidences of biblical record are not admissible, for they cannot believe in the divine preservation of the Bible as a historical record. They would rather invent some deity and name it "Dod" rather than admit the connection with the biblical David.

Thereby, by their own doubt, they propagate that doubt into the populace. In the article mentioned, the authors point out that while Davies' method and query are justified, his conclusions are not substantiated to any persuasive degree.

Satan Tries To Mislead the Masses

The generation that so eagerly espoused atheism was now beginning to realize its folly. There must be some higher order. While atheism was not successful at proving the non-existence of a god, it paved the way for Satan's next assault: the false gospel (the New Age).

This generation found themselves examining new theologies with curious interest. The new (false) gospel offered them a higher order on their own terms. It offered them the benefits of a religion (prosperity, health, etc.) without the commitment (surrender, lifestyle, etc.).

And since the new gospel is packaged (in many cases) to look like Christianity, many people are completely unaware that they are subscribing to a Satanic doctrine.

Satan's Last-Ditch Attack

The very last attack that Satan will launch on the Christian Church will be the advent of the false christ—the antichrist.

The appearance of the antichrist will come at a time when a large part of the population will be looking for some form of a savior. The savior that they seek will be a man who can rule the world and bring order, peace, and prosperity to the earth. They do not seek a savior for their sins. This being the case, the antichrist will fit the bill.

The Millennium Agenda

Chapter 3: Some New Age Philosophies

"If It Feels Good, Do It."

I remember in the 1960s the hippies had several sayings. One of them was "If it feels good, do it." At the time, I believed the phrase to be a reference to their promiscuous lifestyle. But more recently, it has come to symbolize the doctrinal style of the hippies.

New Age philosophy is brimming with feelings. Almost everything is based on feelings.

In contrast, salvation through Jesus is based on faith.

Therefore, since we have been justified through faith, we have peace with God through our Lord Jesus Christ (Romans 5:1 NIV).

This not based on feelings, but faith.

Cafeteria Style Doctrine

We have already discussed several religions of the world. Those were but a few. New Agers afford themselves the luxury of choosing the doctrinal attributes of any religion they wish. Furthermore, they mix and match. They may take spiritualism from the Animists or Shamanists (Native American spiritists) and add some Karma from the Hindu, and then some meditation just for style.

You will find that even some Christians have adopted some New Age blended religion. It's really quite easy to do, and very popular.

The problem is that a corrupted gospel is more deadly than none at all.

If anyone teaches false doctrines and does

> **If anyone teaches false doctrines and does
> not agree to the sound instruction of our
> Lord Jesus Christ and to godly teaching, he
> is conceited and understands nothing. He
> has an unhealthy interest in controversies
> and quarrels about words that result in
> envy, strife, malicious talk, evil suspicions
> and constant friction between men of cor-
> rupt mind, who have been robbed of the
> truth and who think that godliness is a
> means to financial gain (1 Timothy 6:3-5
> NIV).**

All Roads Lead To Heaven

New Agers like to believe that all roads lead to heaven. This is packaged as "tolerance" and "diversity." By allowing everyone the ability to reach heaven in his own way, the New Ager thus ignores his or her own obligation to truth and evangelism. This is one of the most pervasive and popular New Age doctrines.

Jesus was very certain in His declaration of how to reach heaven:

> **Jesus answered, "I am the way and the truth
> and the life. No one comes to the Father
> except through me" (John 14:6 NIV).**

Environmental Responsibility

While this is a worthwhile endeavor, it comes into conflict with the Christian concepts of nature and man's role in conservation.

New Age doctrine places environmental concerns at such a high level that they approach, and in fact, become, nature worship. This is primarily due to the Animistic and Shamanistic influences. These two religions teach that spirits inhabit all things, living or not. Trees and stones all share a spirit, or have a spirit of their own which is to be respected and, in some cases, revered.

The Millennium Agenda

By appeasing these spirits, New Agers gain their place in the universal spirit world. This, of course, ties in with their Karma, and how they hope to be reincarnated.

The Bible tells us that God placed man on earth as a steward of God's creation. That stewardship obligates man to the utmost care and protection of God's creation.

> **Then God said, "Let us make man in our image, in our likeness, and let them rule over the fish of the sea and the birds of the air, over the livestock, over all the earth, and over all the creatures that move along the ground" (Genesis 1:26 NIV).**

Man should make every effort to treat God's creation with the utmost respect. This includes conscientious utilization of resources, but should not be construed to include nature worship.

Self-discovery

Self-discovery is actually part of a curricular method. This teaches children to discover their own solutions. It also discourages teachers from correcting children's mistakes because it may impair their self-discovery.

For instance, teachers will not correct spelling mistakes on a history paper or history errors on a grammar essay paper. In science class, kids are given experiments but not given the expected result.

As innocuous as this may sound, its ulterior motive is for teachers and parents to allow kids to make up their own minds about life decisions, particularly religion. The philosophy is that the child *should* decide on his own what is right for him and not be guided (or persuaded) by the parents' preconceptions. I even saw this philosophy on a poster hanging in the children's section of a church building.

Hopefully you can see the danger in this philosophy. The Bible clearly tells parents to "train a child in the way he should go, and when he is old he will not turn from it" (Proverbs 22:6).

Global Peace

Global peace is a concept which the New Age embraces in a big way. While the Bible tells us that there will not be [global] peace on earth until Christ returns, the New Age teachers believe that man can achieve his own peace. A recurring theme in New Age philosophy is man's interaction with other men, and that the end of that endeavor is world harmony.

Others believe that a christ (not Jesus) will appear to create peace on earth.

> **Jesus answered: "Watch out that no one deceives you. For many will come in my name, claiming, 'I am the Christ,' and will deceive many. You will hear of wars and rumors of wars, but see to it that you are not alarmed. Such things must happen, but the end is still to come. Nation will rise against nation, and kingdom against kingdom. There will be famines and earthquakes in various places. All these are the beginning of birth pains" (Matthew 24:4-8 NIV).**

You Determine Your Own Commitment Level

And to cap it all off, you can simply determine how much or how little you want to participate. New Agers believe that since religion is just a discipline, if you choose not to participate, or if you choose to shave your head and live on a mountain, it is all the same.

Best of all, it means that you can vary your commitment depending on how you feel. If you become busy at work then you simply let religion fall by the wayside. If, on the other hand, you have plenty of time on your hands then you get involved and "act out" your religious duties.

Jesus asked for total commitment. Anything less is a superfluous

The Millennium Agenda

endeavor.

> **Jesus replied: "Love the Lord your God with
> all your heart and with all your soul and
> with all your mind. This is the first and
> greatest commandment" (Matthew 22:37-38
> NIV).**

Moral Relativism

This is the idea that morals are situational. In the Disney movie *Aladdin*, Aladdin steals food but claims that he only steals what he can't afford to buy. The observer is implored to dismiss his crime based on his situation.

In a more practical sense, if you are at a party and meet someone you find attractive, then you can simply forget about moral purity for a while. If you fail to meet a deadline at work and you realize that you could get fired for it, then it's all right for you to lie to save your job. Or, you shouldn't be given a ticket for running the stop sign since you were already late to a meeting.

God's law regarding sin is absolute. Not only absolute, but complete:

> **For whoever keeps the whole law and yet
> stumbles at just one point is guilty of break-
> ing all of it (James 2:10 NIV).**

Relative Evil

"Relative Evil" is a phrase that I coined to describe a common scenario in New Age philosophy. New Age philosophy does not define good and evil in absolute terms. This gives rise to Moral Relativism, for instance. It is based in the Tao concept of Yin Yang, in which good and evil necessarily must co-exist.

A relative evil is a situation where a perceived "good" is in conflict with a perceived "evil." Then, enter another "evil." At this point, the first "evil" and "good" join to battle the extreme evil of the new "evil." Thus, the first "evil" in fact is acting as "good." Once the extreme "evil" is repelled or destroyed, the original "good" and "evil" resume their conflict.

This is an especially common theme in children's cartoons.

What this teaches is that good is not absolute—neither is evil. God is good and He can never tolerate, much less ally, with evil. We are told that the presence of God is like light entering a room. When this happens, all darkness (evil) must leave.

> **In him was life, and that life was the light of men. The light shines in the darkness, but the darkness has not understood it (John 1:4-5 NIV).**

Evolution

No matter what else you believe, as a New Ager, it is important that you accept evolution over creationism. Even if you believe in a god, you must still believe in evolution.

The reason for this is evident in the goal of New Agers. Each New Ager wishes to become something greater than he is. More specifically, he wants to evolve to a higher form. The New Age teaches that this is possible and that the next higher form will be capable of achieving global peace, ending world hunger, and achieving social harmony which is so greatly desired.

The Bible, however, tells us that God created all things, and that Jesus was present at that creation:

> **In the beginning God created the heaven and the earth (Genesis 1:1 KJV).**

> **In the beginning was the Word, and the Word was with God, and the Word was God. The same was in the beginning with God. All things were made by him; and without him was not any thing made that was made (John 1:1-3 KJV).**

The Millennium Agenda

Chapter 4: Evolution

In the last chapter, we talked briefly about evolution. But this is such an integral part of the New Age philosophy that I wanted to spend more time on it.

Evolution is a theory that claims that all living things change for improvement. Evolution claims that the three-toed sloth became three-toed because that is better than a two-toed sloth. Evolution claims that camels decided to grow a hump in order to survive in the desert life.

The Origin of Man

In his book *Origin of Species* (1859), Charles Darwin set forth a proposition of evolution that took the world by storm. He was not the first person to put forth these ideas; however, he has the dubious distinction of being made responsible for them. In fact, Darwin offered several critiques of the ideas that he presented.

In short, evolution claims that life originated from lifeless matter. Further, lower organisms evolved (changed) into higher organisms. This process continues through the advent of modern man.

Now the number of years that are "required" for this to occur are mind-boggling—not thousands, not millions, but billions of years. This does not even account for the time that it supposedly took for the first single cell organisms to animate.

What the New Age philosophy speaks of is far from what Darwin and his contemporaries imagined. The New Age philosophy claims that man (humankind) is on the brink of an evolutionary step.

By now, you may be wondering why we would be talking about an evolutionary step when Darwin postulated millions and billions of years of development. Well, in many fossilized records, there are gaps. In other words, missing links. For instance, from single cell organisms to complex invertebrates, there is no intermediary fossil evidence. From complex invertebrates to lower vertebrates, there is no intermediary fossil evidence. Even between similar animals, there are no fossil remains that account for the differences.

While creationists celebrate this as evidence of creation, evolutionists celebrate this as evidence of evolutionary "jumps." These are periods in which massive and extreme changes occur in such a short time as to leave little or no fossil remains. Keep in mind that a "short time" to an evolutionist is several million years, which Dr. Duane T. Gish, author of *Evolution: The Challenge of the Fossil Record*, claims is ample time for fossil remains to be formed.[10]

Nevertheless, New Agers believe that we are on the brink of the next evolutionary "jump."

A Critique of Evolution

Evolutionists claim that the entire cosmos was formed out of the "Big Bang." They fail, however, to state the origin of the matter which constituted the mass which "banged" into the universe. They prefer to believe that this matter always existed. From this big bang, we see the formation of stars, planets, asteroids, and gaseous clouds. Scientists since Galileo have studied the heavens in great detail. They have found millions and perhaps billions of stars and solar systems.

Scientists have failed at explaining why a singular mass of matter (essentially only electrons) would expand in differing patterns to form planets. In theory, when matter expands in a vacuum (i.e., outer space), it expands uniformly. The only time that the matter would not expand in a uniform pattern would be when acted upon by some force, that force being friction, other matter, or (dare we say) the hand of God.

If, as they claim, the matter (which was totally homogenous) then expanded nonuniformly and formed planets, how would one explain the complex and seemingly unique mixture of chemicals which comprise each planet? In fact, there are a number of factors which must be "just right" in order for life to be possible.[11] Evolutionists answer this by saying that perhaps life of another type would evolve. Well, if this is so, then that "life form" and humans could never coexist, and likely never even interact due to the vastly different circumstances of our "evolution."

But, I digress. The Hubble Space Telescope that was placed in orbit in 1990 was intended to give astronomers a better look at the heavens. This telescope was expected to provide better images of space because it would not be subject to the atmospheric distortions that we experience in earthbound telescopes.

The telescope had a minor (but costly) problem that required correction before it could produce the imagery expected. After that, scientists quickly hailed that they had discovered the origin of the universe. Actually, what they had done was determine that the universe (as Einstein postulated) was expanding. In fact, it was expanding from a central point. And furthermore, assuming a constant (or at least, a known) rate of expansion (no friction), they could estimate the "point" at which matter would have been a singular mass. (It's like running a film in reverse to find out how a movie began.)

What they concluded was that the universe could be no more than "several billion years old."[12] The irony here is that evolutionists claim the earth itself to be about 4.5 billions years old.[13] The age of the earth was determined using radiometric dating methods. This makes the earth roughly the same age as the universe. This does not allow for the formation of the solar system and stabilization of the earth's orbit, etc.

Furthermore, many fossil remains exist which have prompted evolutionists to proclaim evolution. The only problem is that there are no transitional forms. As we discussed earlier, we have fossils of single cell organisms, and fossils of complex invertebrates, but nothing in between. There are no fossil remains of any transitional forms.

In fact, all the fossils that we can find, regardless of geologic age, are simply the same organism, or another variety of the same species. We have, for instance, fossils of apes and fossils of

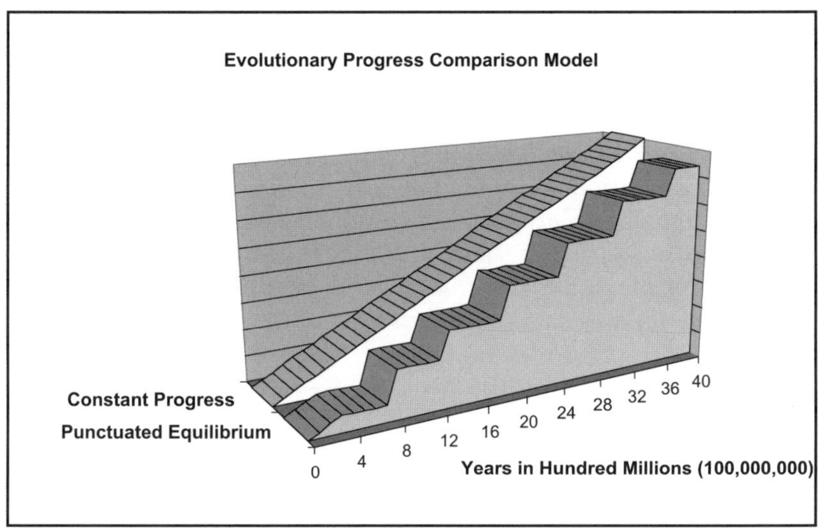

humanoids, but no evidence that is in between the two. This means that while evolutionists represent all life as originating from a single source (i.e., single cell organisms), and advancing in complexity to man, there is no fossil evidence to suggest any relationships between species. This mere fact supports a creationist's view. The Bible tells us that God created all things in stages—in different and distinct periods of time.

Scientists evade this fact by introducing the theory of punctuated equilibrium. This theory published by Niles Eldredge and Stephen Jay Gould states that "species tend to remain stable for long periods, only to undergo bursts of rapid evolution."[14] In essence, they claim that since we have no evidence of transitional forms, the transitions must have happened quite rapidly—so rapid, in fact, that there is no fossil evidence remaining from them. In short, the absence of evidence proves the fact. Preposterous!

The diagram above illustrates the comparison of evolutionary progress. The slope in the background illustrates the relatively constant (classical) evolutionary progress. The slope in the foreground illustrates the principle of punctuated equilibrium in which evolution occurs in bursts of relatively quick steps only to

The Millennium Agenda

remain stable for long periods.

The evolutionists' claim that life began out of inanimate matter is based on the potential presence of amino acids in nature resulting from natural phenomena. It is true that scientists can mix up a chemical concoction of common elements, add some energy—say a thunderstorm—and produce some amino acids. This discovery made them ecstatic, but the reality is that amino acid, while essential for life, is not itself life. Nor does it necessarily give rise to life.

Now before we go much further, let's talk about Genesis, Chapter 1. Scholars do not agree on the time span in which creation occurred. The Hebrew word *yowm* is used in Chapter 1 of Genesis to depict the periods of creation. The word is interpreted as "day" in English. This usage of the word typically depicts a single rotation of the earth: a 24-hour period. Keep in mind that God created for three "days" before He created the sun. Thus, measuring the creation based on a rotation of the earth with respect to our sun, which had not yet been created, does not make sense.

Interestingly, though, light and darkness were separated and thus called "day" and "night" on the first day. On the fourth day, the sun and moon were created.

Many scholars prefer to think (and I agree) of the word *yowm* as representative of "era." This usage is consistent with other uses of the word *yowm* in other parts of the Old Testament. This, then, allows for the expanses of time which fossil remains apparently indicate without compromising the biblical truth of creation.

Let me further state that I do not pretend to understand the intricacies of *how* God created the universe and all life. I accept, on faith, that God in His wisdom created life with specific goals and purposes in mind.

There is a second thought that I would like to impart. Most fossil dating is accomplished using a process commonly known as carbon dating. This process is quite complex; however, in simple terms, it measures the levels of carbon in an object. Life on earth is carbon based. That means that carbon is an essential element of our chemical structure. Plants use water, air, and carbon to form sugar. Since plants do not need energy to move, they can absorb light energy and turn the basic elements of hydrogen, oxygen, and carbon into carbohydrates. Humans and animals eat plants and in humans and animals, those carbohydrates (sugars) are broken down back into their basic elements (hydrogen, oxygen, and carbon). This transformation releases energy with which we move, speak, and think.

When a living organism dies, its level of carbon dissipates. Carbon dating assumes that the dissipation rate is known and constant. This may or may not be true. Consider the dissipation models.

In the Linear Dissipation Model, notice that the dissipation occurs on a straight gradient from 20 to 0. For our example, this occurs over 20,000 years. (Keep in mind, these charts are merely examples and are not intended to demonstrate scientific evidence or actual carbon dissipation.)

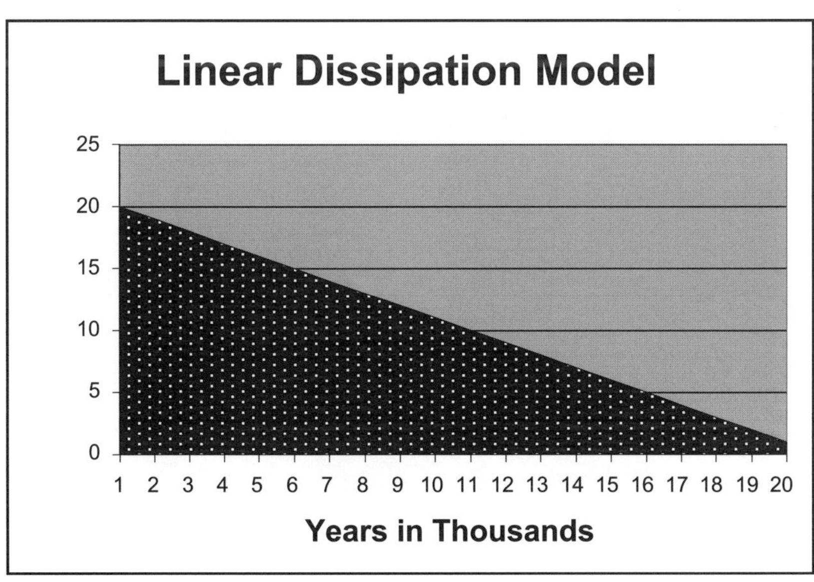

The Millennium Agenda

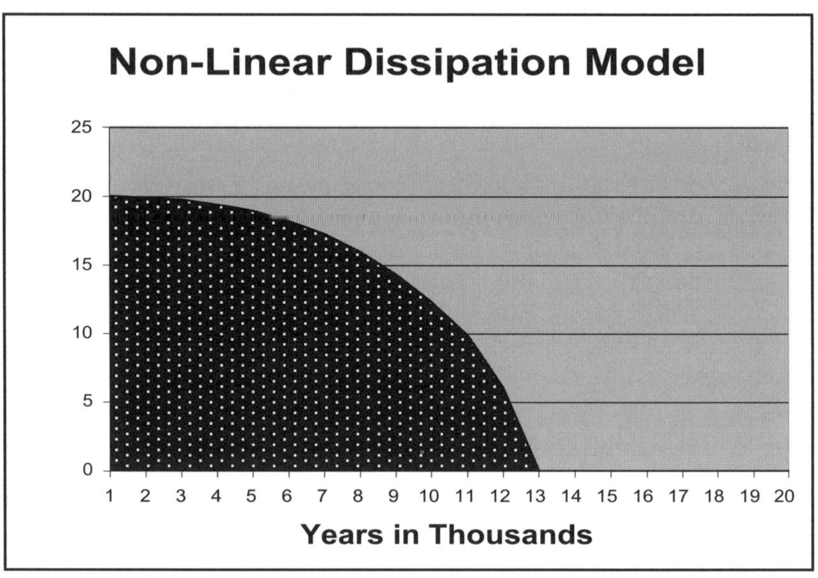

In the Non-Linear Dissipation Model, we see that the dissipation begins gradually, but then accelerates until the total carbon is dissipated in about two-thirds the time.

Carbon dating is (in paleontological terms) very new. In fact, we have only a few thousand years of artifacts which can be historically dated with which to "calibrate" our carbon dating. Beyond that, scientists have no idea how carbon dissipation actually occurs.

Suffice it to say, then, that carbon dating may not be as accurate as scientists would like us to believe. But that can never be proved or disproved.

Chapter 5: Evolution II

Since the New Age is based on evolution, it is necessary to take the discussion to the next level. How does this tie into today's events?

Well, since we are (according to evolutionists) evolving, then we must constantly be in a state of change. Even though we appear to be in a static form, we are, in fact, changing. Just as we look on the horizon and perceive it to be flat, so we also perceive ourselves as unchanging in the larger scheme of evolution. We do not appear to be changing, nor can we perceive any evidence of change. But from a removed point of view, we can see the complete sphere of the earth, or, as evolutionists would like to believe, we could see the complete progression of evolution.

From time to time, people have claimed to be privy to our evolutionary path. And as evolution claims, we must be evolving to a higher state. To what higher state could we be evolving? Science fiction writers and movies have pictured hairless humans with huge heads having telepathic and telekinetic powers. The sad thing is that New Agers see the same picture. Maybe not the huge head, but the god-like powers of omniscience and omnipotence.

The Man I Could Be...

Now, let's examine what the next evolutionary level would be. Helena Blavatsky wrote a book called *The Secret Doctrine* in the 19th century. Blavatsky was, for all intents and purposes, a Satanist. Her book, although nearly all plagiarized from other writers, received much recognition. The book went into great detail about the evolution of man and what man would become. Blavatsky claimed that man is now in the Aquarian age. (Upon reading this, a chill ran down my spine as I recalled the song from the 1960s, "The Age of Aquarius.") She further claims that the next age will be the Aryan age. This also sent chills down my spine as I recalled that Hitler was seeking the Aryan race of men to rule the world.

Hitler, in fact, kept Blavatsky's book at his bedside. He was very

The Millennium Agenda

familiar with it and was intent on bringing about the Aryan age.
He, of course, saw himself as the leader of the Aryan race.

Hitler strongly incorporated the principles of evolution into his
campaign. He took the concept and applied it to sociology. This is
how he justified many of his programs. It is commonly known
that Hitler also subscribed to the philosophies of Immanuel Kant
and Georg Wilhelm Friedrich Hegel. Kant proposed that God, if
there was any, was totally unperceivable and thus "reality" was
merely what man perceived it to be. This gives rise to Moral
Relativism.

Hegel refuted the idea of thesis and antithesis (absolute
opposites). He claimed that those things that appear to be
opposite are really *becoming* one new thing. For instance, there is
no black and white, because they are becoming gray. This gives
rise to Relative Evil. In this concept, "evil" and "good" are not
necessarily opposing forces, because they will synthesize to
produce something new, which will in turn find another
"opposite." This is known as the Hegelian Dialect.

> **Hegel's dialectic logic obliterates the ideas of
> an objective God, of absolute truth, and of
> moral absolutes.**[15]

Let's talk a little more about the Aryan race. This race, according
to Blavatsky and New Age philosophers, will have super intellect,
telepathic ability, telekinetic abilities, and so forth. This being
the case, all those wishing to catch the next train to the Aryan
race should study up on these techniques. This means that one
should perform seances to enhance telepathic skills, utilize
visualization and meditation exercises for telekinetic skills, and
brisk secular (paranormal) discussion to enhance the intellect.

These, of course, introduce the participant (unwittingly) to the
occult. The participant, who swears off religion since he is "open
minded," and a "free thinker," embraces the religion of the occult
without even realizing that he has done it.

Participants find themselves performing all sorts of ridiculous
religious (and pagan) rituals in order to become "enlightened," but

they will not cross the street to walk in a Christian church.

Interesting Parallels

John Whitehead, in his book *The Stealing of America*, spends a great deal of effort drawing parallels between pre-World War II German sociology and current American sociology. His book was copyrighted in 1983 and his predictions have not been as prompt as he suggests; however, his conclusions are quite interesting.

The philosophies of Kant and Hegel became very popular in Germany. German society was considered to be a model society. However, this swank and admired society had an unknown agenda brewing. Basing their sociological views on Kant and Hegel, individuals became less and less responsible for their own actions. Rather, when a criminal committed a crime, it was considered a problem of society rather than of the individual. The society was examined for a remedy, and the criminal was treated, rehabilitated, and released.

The greater effect of this is that individuals no longer were responsible for actions of the government. That is, the society, as a whole, acted. Hitler stated that the individual ego is of "no importance in comparison with the existence of his nation."[16] This philosophy is collectivism or as we currently call it, socialism.

Combine this with evolution, and the holocaust becomes a mere informality on Germany's road to supremacy. In his book, Whitehead states:

> **Under this philosophy [collectivism] all life became relative. If, as it did, it became convenient to exterminate people at Auschwitz, it was done. This was still easier to do with evolution as a foundation. After all, man is yet an evolving animal.**
>
> **The Jews, labeled subhumans, became nonbeings. It was both legal and right to exterminate them.**[17]

We have all heard the stories of how the German citizens stood by and watched as the Jews were slaughtered. The man who sold the cyanide for the gas chambers simply claimed that if he hadn't sold the cyanide, then someone else would have. Individuals felt exonerated under the guise and umbrella of society.

And one could hardly call the German citizens ignorant of Hitler's plans. The society was becoming more and more secular, and in fact more deeply involved in the occult. The populace had so embraced the idea of evolution that the proposals and claims of Hitler were not only accepted, but also welcomed and sanctioned by the public. After all, Hitler, the head of the Nazi party, was voted as President and Chancellor of Germany by an 88 percent vote. The public was well aware of the Nazi party's agenda and claims.

Now let's get back to American society. Today, if a crime is committed, the criminal's rights are protected to such a degree that the victim is further injured by the state. The criminal is not held entirely accountable for his actions. Lawyers examine the circumstances to determine if society imposed undue stress on the defendant. And if so, perhaps his sentence should be reduced, or eliminated.

Furthermore, we can see a strong influence of evolutionary doctrine in our country. While I do not have time here to go into all the details of this parallel, suffice it to say that society in America today is very similar to that of pre-war Germany. For more details see Whitehead's book.

The Next Evolutionary Jump

New Agers believe, as did Hitler, that we are on the brink of an evolutionary jump. Remember that this is when evolutionists claim evolutionary advances occur over a short period of time. They believe that the next evolutionary jump will occur within this generation. In fact, many believe that the next jump will occur sometime shortly after the year 2000.

This is peculiar in that many ancient calendars such as the Aztec and Egyptian calendars end within a generation after 2000. The Aztec calendar, for instance, simply ends. So does the ancient

Egyptian calendar, and others. Why? The ancient calendars are based on cycles and the cycles simply stop. This is a difficult concept for modern people to grasp, because our calendar is based on a starting point and simply counts indefinitely.

Ancient calendars all marked time in cycles. The Gregorian calendar, for example, utilizes these familiar cycles:

    7 days = 1 week
    4 weeks = 1 month (lunar)
    13 months (lunar) = 1 year
    10 years = decade

The cycle of largest scope of the ancient calendars completes shortly after the year 2000.

Evolutionists and New Agers believe that this abrupt end in the ancient calendars is evidence of an imminent evolutionary jump. The idea of an evolutionary jump being observable around the year 2000, or even over several generations afterward, is simply preposterous. An evolutionary jump (if it exists) would have to

The Aztec Calendar Stone supposedly calculates the end of time. According to the calendar, the earth will be destroyed in a catastrophe of fire. Also, according to the calendar, in an earlier period the earth ended in destruction by global flood.

In the Aztec calendar, there are 20 periods of 13 days. Certain combinations of these days are lucky or unlucky. Tribe members born on certain days were destined to be human sacrifices. Multiples were also significant.

The Millennium Agenda

occur over many thousands, if not millions, of years. Again, in paleontological terms, a million years is a *short time*. The passing of a hundred years, in evolutionary terms, is insignificant. If an evolutionary jump did occur, no single human could live long enough to witness its completion.

In conclusion, let me state that evolution builds a basis for racism. It literally claims that some individuals are better (more evolved) than others (less evolved). And as you might expect, white-Anglo persons are considered the more evolved followed by olive, tan, and ruddy complexioned and finally by black skinned people. I find this highly ironic in an age when we are (supposedly) trying to eliminate racism. And at the same time, evolution is taught as fact in our schools.

The life of Jesus is an example of how we should treat others. This means people of all races and backgrounds. Recall the Samaritan woman with whom Jesus spoke. The disciples walked around the town to avoid the Samaritans. Jesus ministered to the woman without regard for her origin. Jesus treated the beggars with the same respect as the wealthy. He loved the weak just as much as the strong. And, He died for all sinners alike.

Section II

Common New Age Manifestations

The Millennium Agenda

Chapter 6: Angel Contact

Angels and stories of angels have become very popular lately. We all like to think that we have our own guardian angel. Many people claim to have contact with angels. The number of movies, TV shows, and books on angels is at an all-time high. Bookstores now feature entire sections dealing only with angels.

The New Age movement, however, has changed how we think about angels.

Let's examine what the New Age angels are telling us. New Age angels have (supposedly) communicated a variety of information to man. There are some authors who claim that angels have told them how the world was created, and how the world will end. But usually angels will have some "religious" spin on what they say.

It is not uncommon to hear the name of Jesus when reading or hearing some angel account. In fact, it is rare when Jesus is not mentioned. But the message that the angels convey is confusing. Almost all angel accounts seem to downplay Jesus' role in man's salvation. They teach a doctrine of love. This doctrine teaches that we should love everyone and simply accept them for who and what they are. We should not judge people or try to change them.

This doctrine is also known as "tolerance" and "diversity."

The New Age angels interact with humans at their own discretion. They help someone in harm's way, they convey future events, and convey religious "truths." But, these "angels" also may use their powers for evil purposes.

An Internet site about angels featured a short story about angels titled "Angels and Children." It was written by Mimi Walch Doe. The Internet site says of Ms. Doe:

> **[Ms.] Doe holds a Masters in Education from Harvard. She has changed the way hundreds of adults interact with children through her workshops on SPIRITUAL PARENTING.**[18]

In the short story, Ms. Doe records the account of her then four-year-old daughter's encounter with an angel:

> **Sophine is the angel who comes to my room each night.**[19]

The name "Sophine" may be a variation of the Greek word *sophia* which means wisdom. New Age messengers and themes are often associated with knowledge or wisdom. The child further explains:

> **I was also an angel before I was born. I watched over you and I picked you to be my mommy. I knew Sophine then and she comes to me now.**[20]

The author then adds:

> **Children do seem to see and experience angels in a vivid and personal way. Validating children's spiritual connection has become my passion. They are still connected with the world so many of us have forgotten. Angels, as one child told me, could make everybody happy if only people would listen.**[21]

She finishes by explaining that her daughter, at eight, had a new angel:

> **He was in the kitchen last night and again this morning on the deck with his strong, loving wings around the house.**[22]

The popular notion is that angels are like people, having the same will and discretion. They have no apparent directive.

In contrast, however, angels in the Bible have a specific purpose. The Bible mentions angels nearly 300 times. In each instance, holy angels carry out the express will of God. There are actually two other types of heavenly beings mentioned: seraphim and cherubim. Neither cherubim nor seraphim are described as having human characteristics. Angels, on the other hand, are always described as men and were created to do the bidding of God. They are servants. They desire only to serve God. They never draw attention to themselves but give glory to God. They

The Millennium Agenda

are spiritual beings; however, they can take on material form in order to minister to or interact with humans. Their only interaction with humans is to carry out a specific mission. As far as guardian angels, the Bible says that God "will command his angels concerning you to guard you in all your ways" (Psalm 91:11).

The rare accounts where angels act autonomously are when the angel is specifically identified as the "angel of the Lord." This is almost universally believed to be Jesus pre-incarnate.

> **The angel of the Lord first appeared to Hagar when she fled from Sarai's wrath (Genesis 16:7). The angel of the Lord encountered heroes of faith such as Abraham (Genesis 22:11-18), Moses (Exodus 3:2) and Gideon (Judges 6:12-22). Sometimes the angel of the Lord seems to speak for God in first person, and those to whom He appeared thought they had seen God Himself.[23]**

The apostle John encountered an angel while receiving the Revelation. At one point, John bows to give worship to the angel:

> **Then the angel said to me, "Write: 'Blessed are those who are invited to the wedding supper of the Lamb!' " And he added, "These are the true words of God."**

> **At this I fell at his feet to worship him. But he said to me, "Do not do it! I am a fellow servant with you and with your brothers who hold to the testimony of Jesus. Worship God! For the testimony of Jesus is the spirit of prophecy" (Revelation 19:9-10 NIV).**

This angel acted consistently with the gospel.

Evil angels, or demons, want to overthrow the gospel. They want to deceive and destroy. Satan and his angels were cast out of heaven due to his sin. Even now, Satan uses his angels to interact with humans in order to confuse the gospel message and mislead people. He wants you to believe in a watered-down gospel. He wants you to believe that his demons are holy angels. He wants you to believe that you do not need Jesus.

In his letter to the Colossians, Paul addressed a practice that was common—that of angel worship.

> **Do not let anyone who delights in false humility and the worship of angels disqualify you for the prize. Such a person goes into great detail about what he has seen, and his unspiritual mind puffs him up with idle notions.**
>
> **He has lost connection with the Head, from whom the whole body, supported and held together by its ligaments and sinews, grows as God causes it to grow (Colossians 2:18-19 NIV).**

Paul explains that people who worship (give reverence to) angels have lost touch with the real Head of the Church which is Christ.

I came across an Internet site in which a woman claimed to be a witch and worshiped angels. As part of her ritual, she would build a shrine of candles and incense and occasionally serve angel food cake. My wife commented that devil's food cake would be more appropriate.

Do Angels Have Wings?

According to the Bible, they do not. Seraphim and cherubim do have wings, but angels are never described with wings. In fact, the idea of angels with wings began in early Christian art. In paintings and drawings, angels were given wings to distinguish them from human figures.

This being the case, it makes me curious why so many angel accounts today describe angels with wings. Since every account of angels in the Bible mentions no outstanding features about angels (other than human form), I must conclude that their appearance would be that of a human.

The Millennium Agenda

On the other hand, cherubim and seraphim are almost always described as having wings. In describing the construction of the ark of the covenant, Moses was instructed regarding the cherubim. The following scripture is God's instruction to Moses concerning the cherubim and their placement on the ark of the covenant:

> **And the cherubims shall stretch forth their wings on high, covering the mercy seat with their wings, and their faces shall look one to another; toward the mercy seat shall the faces of the cherubims be (Exodus 25:20 KJV).**

Samuel described a cherubim in a psalm recorded in Second Samuel:

> **And he rode upon a cherub, and did fly: and he was seen upon the wings of the wind (2 Samuel 22:11 KJV).**

In First Kings, we are given the description of the cherubim that were to be in the temple that Solomon built:

> **In the inner sanctuary he made a pair of cherubim of olive wood, each ten cubits high. One wing of the first cherub was five cubits long, and the other wing five cubits— ten cubits from wing tip to wing tip (1 Kings 6:23-24 NIV).**

Isaiah describes seraphim in a vision:

> **Above it stood the seraphims: each one had six wings; with twain he covered his face, and with twain he covered his feet, and with twain he did fly (Isaiah 6:2 KJV).**

Note that cherubim have two wings, while seraphim have six wings.

Chapter 7: Alien Contact

How many recent movies, TV shows, books, and magazines have featured aliens? You can't even check out your groceries without seeing some tabloid with a claim about aliens or alien contact. The New Age movement asserts that aliens are creatures who have evolved to a higher state than humans. These aliens come to earth to help humans evolve to their next, higher state.

The Search for Extraterrestrial Intelligence

Scientists all over the world study the sky for signs of other life. The United States spent billions of dollars on the Hubble space telescope. This telescope searches deep into space with unprecedented clarity. But the fact is that scientists have never spotted any UFO outside the earth's atmosphere.

In July 1971, Astronaut David Scott of Apollo 15.[24]

In the 1960s the United States, led by President Kennedy's vision, was poised to launch a major program to put a man on the moon. This was achieved in 1969 and by this time, the United States had planned for an unprecedented voyage into outer space. The spacecraft *Voyager* was launched at a time when the planets were aligned. NASA sent the space probe tumbling toward outer space carrying a message of peace for whomever it would encounter. On board the spacecraft was a gold-plated copper phonograph record. Carl Sagan described the record:

> **Since, after its exploration of the giant planets, the two Voyager spacecraft will leave the solar system, they bear messages for any interstellar civilization that may come upon them. The record jacket gives in scientific notation, instructions for playing the record and something of the position and present epoch of the Earth. The record itself**

The Millennium Agenda

will last for a billion years.[25]

On April 24, 1964, police officer Lonnie Zamora spotted an unusual light while pursuing a speeding car. He broke his pursuit with the speeding car and went to where he saw the light. At that place, he claims to have seen a spaceship and two figures. The spaceship then lifted off, hovered, and sped off at breakneck speed. That place was Socorro, New Mexico.

The investigation of Zamora's claim is said to be "one of the most thoroughly investigated of all UFO cases, and though it depends almost wholly on the testimony of one percipient, it stands as one of the classic sightings."[27]

In the desert of Socorro, New Mexico, there are dozens of radio telescopes that scan the vast expanse for some sign of intelligence from space. Amid all this tomfoolery, one wonders if maybe scientists should be searching for signs of intelligence among their own ranks.

Radio Telescopes of Socorro, New Mexico. Operated by the National Radio Astronomy Observatory.[26]

The primary reason for the space mission to Mars in the mid-1990s was to look for signs of life on Mars. The U.S. government funded (through NASA) the Mars mission. Many Americans watched as the little rover-craft bumped into rocks and pointed cameras at the Martian terrain. It found some ice.

Scientists claim that the presence of ice means that the Martian surface may have once been partially covered with water. They extend this to conclude that the presence of water introduces the chance of life on the surface of Mars. In December of 1999, a probe was landed on the south pole of Mars—the location of the ice. I have no doubt that this probe's mission was to explore that ice and surrounding area for signs of primitive life forms, past or present. NASA engineers lost radio contact with the probe just minutes before touchdown and have not been able to determine its fate.

There are some formations on the surface of Mars that many claim could only have been created by intelligent beings. While scientists and amateur astrologists can make all kinds of speculation about the odd formations and presence of water, they still have no evidence of life. A *Newsweek* article reported:

> **With the report last month that life may have gained a toehold on Mars 3.5 billion years ago, space scientists suddenly have a good reason to look more carefully at blueprints for getting humans to Mars.***[28]

The author continues that the life, ever so primitive, must have been driven underground by whatever cataclysm made the surface uninhabitable. This being the case, it is unlikely that any robot on the surface could detect that life. Further, robots could not successfully explore below the Martian surface.

The Very Large Array (VLA) is one of the world's premier astronomical radio observatories. The VLA consists of 27 antennas arranged in the huge Y pattern up to 36km (22 miles) across, with the sensitivity of a dish 130 meters (422 feet) in diameter.[30]

The Millennium Agenda

Paleontologist Jack Farmer of NASA's Ames Research Center in California states that:

> **Exploring below the Martian surface for water and living microorganisms may provide the most compelling reasons for carrying out human missions to Mars.**[29]

This is saying that the only reason to send humans to Mars is to find life—not to determine if there are exploitable resources, or if the planet could become habitable, but to *find life*—to prove evolution. And why is NASA employing a paleontologist? Paleontology is "the study of the forms of life existing in prehistoric or geologic times, as represented by the fossils of plants, animals, and other organisms."[31] It sounds like NASA exists for more that just space exploration—it exists in order to prove evolution.

The recent movie "Mission to Mars" fantasizes about scientists discovering the secrets of life on Mars.

Who Are They?

What do we really know about aliens? In the midst of all the rumors and speculation about aliens, there is still no rock-hard evidence that they exist.

According to United States Air Force statistics, nearly four million Americans claim to have been abducted by aliens. During the abduction, the abductees are examined physically, are usually unable to control their own motor activity (can't move), and are subjected to physical invasion (probes up the nostril, abdomen, etc.). Most of these encounters end with the victim returned otherwise unharmed to the place of origin.

An Internet site that is devoted to UFO abduction claims:

> **"Abductee" is the term most recognized by the public. As abductees learn more about their abduction experiences, many prefer to be called contactees, experiencers, or participants.**

This shift in terminology often reflects the abductees' change in attitude from fear to acceptance. They accept it because they feel they cannot change the phenomena. They are a product of it and will live with its effects. Or, they may feel compelled to learn more about their abduction experience by meeting with other abductees and working with researchers.[32]

Many people claim to have had conversations with aliens. These conversations take place either in face-to-face situations or through meditation or channeling. Like angel contact, people who talk to aliens receive information about the origin of life on earth, Lucifer, Jesus, and other religious topics. I am not sure why aliens would be at all concerned with religious topics on Earth since they are supposedly not from Earth.

Nevertheless, some people claim that Lucifer (according to the aliens) is a misunderstood alien; that he was only looking to help "enlighten" the man and woman in the Garden of Eden. Having done so, other aliens, out of anger, convinced the people that Lucifer was evil. Furthermore, they claim that Lucifer comes again today to "enlighten" the human race, but the pious religious (Christian) relic of the past is inhibiting this progress.

Others claim that Satan, Lucifer, and Yahweh are all one in the same and that this being has realized the error of his ways and is no longer evil. Proponents of this claim invite us to welcome this bringer of light.[33]

There are even some who believe that Jesus is the commander of a space ship that now orbits Earth and that He reports to Lucifer. The bottom line is that there is a lot of distorted information about Jesus.

The name "Lucifer" means "bringer of light," or "morning star." Isn't it interesting that the New Age movement refers to knowledge as "light."

The Millennium Agenda

Chariots of the Gods

Do you remember *Chariots of the Gods?* This was a book by Erich Von Däniken that was followed by a movie which claimed that ancient Central and South American and Egyptian hieroglyphs depicted alien creatures. Von Däniken claims that these aliens instructed the ancient humans on such architectural feats as the pyramids. This gave rise, claims Von Däniken, to religions. He states that these humans perceived the aliens to be gods because of their superior knowledge:

> **All over the world there are ruins and im-
> probable objects which cannot be explained
> by conventional theories of archeology or
> religion. But supposing you look at them in
> the light of today's knowledge about space
> travel. A remarkable consistency emerges.
> They suggest the appearance of beings from
> other planets in prehistoric times and pose
> the question—Was God an Astronaut?**[34]

Von Däniken claims that he was given this knowledge through telepathy with "an unknown source" and "out-of-body travels."

Von Däniken suggested that humans were really placed on Earth and nurtured by aliens somewhat like planting flowers in a desert.

So why do so many people believe this? Author William Alnor says:

> **People want to believe in
> ancient astronauts
> because it absolves them
> of their responsibility to
> their creator. It gives
> them an out, and most
> people will take it every
> time.**[35]

The Giza pyramids in Egypt.

It is interesting to note that Von Däniken "had multiple convictions in Swiss courts for fraud and embezzlement, and during one of the proceedings, a court-appointed psychiatrist pronounced him a 'pathological liar' and a 'psychopath.'"[36]

Another author said of Von Däniken's theory regarding the immense ground markings in Peru:

Pyramid in Chichen Itza, Mexico

> **But while few scientists would deny the charm of Von Däniken's story, fewer still lend it credence.**[37]

At the age of about ten, I came across a book entitled *The Stranger at the Pentagon*. My grandmother had acquired the book and read it. She was apparently impressed with Stranges' credentials (see below) and presented my father with the book. I read the book and even at the age of ten I found its claims preposterous.

The author, Frank E. Stranges, Ph.D. (what a name), claims that in 1959 he had access to the Pentagon and was led to a secret room where he met "Val Thor" (Val short for Valiant). Val Thor claimed (according to Stranges) to be from Venus, very familiar with the Bible, and sinless. Stranges' book also goes to great lengths to prove, or at least add great plausibility to, the existence of alien life.

An introduction to the book contains the following statement:

> **This testimony is for the benefit of all Earth people. If you believe this really happened, then it is true. If you do not believe it happened, just treat it...as a novel.**[38]

I have trouble understanding how a testimony can be either fact or fiction at the discretion of the reader. Another section of the book is written in the first person of Val Thor and describes an encounter with an investigator:

> **We discussed the merits of Jesus Christ.**

The Millennium Agenda

> **How He gave His life freely – so that men could enjoy the benefits of eternal life. He questioned me as to the Bible on Venus. I assured him that a personal unbroken fellowship with the "Author" did not necessitate the printing of a "book."**[39]

In this passage, Stranges (or Val Thor, if you please) suggests that Jesus resides on Venus.

Stranges claims to be a Christian.   And what's even more peculiar is that Stranges' message emphasizes a belief in Jesus as exclusive Lord. In the New Age arena, he stands alone in this emphasis.   Stranges has served as president of the International Evangelism Crusades Inc., and director of Instructors of Faith Bible College & Theological Seminary in Fort Lauderdale, Florida (from which he received his Bachelor of Divinity, Doctor of Psychology, and Doctor of Philosophy degrees).

However, amid all the Christianity, one must still question the validity and objective of Stranges' message. Val Thor, Stranges claims, has come to help humans find the way back to the saving grace of Jesus. Why would God send a Venusian to minister to humans? And why would a prophet be named "Thor" after the Norse (pagan) god of thunder? And why would Val Thor claim to be from a planet that we now know is totally inhospitable to any life that we could imagine?

At the Movies

Now what do television shows and movies about aliens have to do with anything? For starters, they desensitize the viewer. Desensitization is a process in which you become increasingly comfortable with an idea simply by repeated exposure to it. Take for instance, TV violence: on first seeing a graphic scene of violence on TV, you might have felt anxious, uncomfortable, or even disturbed. However, if you watch the same sort of violence repeatedly, you will reach a point where these scenes have little or no effect on you. The same is true with shows about aliens. In the '50s, we all laughed at the garish special effects in science fiction movies. Now, due to the incredible technology of the computer, it is difficult to know when something is "real" or not. The point is that the American public has become so accustomed to the idea of aliens that most people would tell you they do believe in aliens—not because they have seen them, or talked to them, or even that they know someone who has. They will believe in aliens simply because they have been bombarded with "alienology" for the greater part of their lives in movies and television. Furthermore, have you noticed how the alien presence has changed? In the '50s, aliens came to Earth to destroy life as we know it. In *War of the Worlds* the aliens were determined to destroy all human life. There was no apparent purpose, just destruction.

However, in the last decade, aliens have come to bring peace, health, happiness, and a better life to Earth. Remember *Close Encounters of the Third Kind*? The aliens, although clearly of superior intelligence, are harmless and somewhat curious. Note also that they telepathically communicated with humans to announce their arrival. They even telepathically select certain individuals to herald or even champion their arrival.

In the movies *Cocoon* and *Cocoon II*, the aliens have such miraculous healing power that they allow several convalescent senior citizens to join them in their journey and thus gain near immortality. In the recent movie *Contact*, aliens wanted to contact humans. They instructed humans on how to build a spacecraft capable of reaching them.

Note that in the above examples, and as a common recurring theme, aliens are depicted as light, radiant beings. This is also consistent with my conclusion below.

Perhaps the only exception to the benevolent alien theme is the recent movie *Independence Day*. In this movie, we are faced with the "reality" that aliens have the power and inclination to exact "judgment" on the human race.

So, why is alien judgment on humans significant? This may be the most eye-opening question in this book. In an episode of the original *Star Trek*, Captain Kirk and his team of specialists

The Millennium Agenda

descend to a planet in which the inhabitants are less evolved than Kirk and his crew. Although they were less evolved, they were close enough that Kirk and his crew had the ability and means to help advance the society.

After multiple and determined protests by the orthodox religious group on the planet, Kirk and crew return to the *Enterprise* frustrated. They were not able to help the inhabitants because of the orthodox religious group who refused to depart from the "old ways." The orthodox religious leaders of the planet believed that even though the society could evolve, they would lose necessary religious structure. The religious leaders believed that the society should progress at its own pace in order to maintain the continuity of the religion.

The moral, in case you missed it, is a parallel to how the New Age sees Christians. New Agers believe that we are on the brink of an evolutionary jump and that the aliens have come to assist us. Christians will stand in the way of this advance because of its association with the New Age (which relegates the role of Jesus to just a good human). For this reason, Christians will be hated and ostracized.

One author summed up the philosophical nature of the *Enterprise* like this:

> **In the continuing adventures aboard the good ship *Enterprise*, there is an entire belief system so complete, so compelling, and so powerful that it literally represents the greatest alternative to the Gospel that has ever been offered to mankind.**[40]

The author, Peter Lalonde, continues:

> **In the *Star Trek* future, human worldy problems have been solved, and generally, everyone seems to get along very well.**[41]

This being the case, New Agers believe that aliens will cleanse (remove all Christians from) Earth prior to the evolutionary jump. This will be necessary to remove the opposition prior to the action of advancement. The aliens will have both the means and inclination to carry out this cleansing (judgment).

I hope you have realized the parallel of this event to the rapture. Lalonde adds that, as in *Star Trek*,

> **The transporter beam gives the world a context for people disappearing right before their very eyes.**[42]

This is exactly what the Bible says will happen, that Christians will be transformed, that is, taken up in the twinkling of an eye.

> **[The transporter beam] will be the only frame of reference that [non-Christians] will have.**[43]

So, when the rapture happens, the people who remain on earth will not be startled and confused, but rather surprised and re-lieved. Those who remain, rather than reflect on what the Bible says about the rapture, will be more familiar with the New Age act of cleansing and will be convinced, in that moment, that the aliens have cleansed the earth and that advancement is immi-nent.

In Religion

While looking for some research material at the local library, I ran across a book titled *Visitors From Outer Space*. It was from a series entitled *The Supernatural*.*

I thought the book might have some interesting information in it. I was shocked to find the baphomet (inverted pentagram) on the inside leaf. This symbol is characteristic of satanic worship. See Chapter 8 for more information on the symbol.

The book contained much of the same type of information that I had already gathered, with one exception. Chapter 4 of the book was entitled "Spacecraft in Early Times." This chapter attempted to explain oddities and unidentified celestial objects from myths,

---

*The Supernatural: The Danbury Press; A Division of Grolier Enterprises Inc.

71

legends, and historical accounts. Of particular interest was the interpretation of some biblical events. The author states that the star that guided the three wise men to the location of the infant Jesus was an alien spacecraft. He further explains that the three wise men were analogous to our "men in black" that are rumored to surface at each UFO sighting.

The author further concludes that the aerial craft that Ezekiel described (in Chapter 1 of Ezekiel) was in fact a humanoid alien that had emblems with figures of an eagle, lion, and bull. The figures that Ezekiel saw are identified as cherubim in Chapter 10 of Ezekiel. The author also states that the reason Moses saw a burning bush was because an alien spacecraft was hovering over the bush and belched flames into it.

These conclusions were even confirmed (in the book) by a pastor. My interest now piqued, I looked for what kind of "pastor" this might be. He was identified as "Barry L. Downing, pastor of Northminster Presbyterian Church in Endwell, New York."[44]

Conclusions

Satan wants to deceive humanity. He will spare no effort to create some hope for humankind other than the saving grace of Jesus Christ. The concept of aliens creates the sense that humankind can somehow rise to a better life by its own devices. Interestingly, people who claim to have talked to aliens all say the same thing: the aliens promise a better life for humanity.

Scripture warns us to be on guard against deception. Paul warned about the "angels of light" sent by Satan to deceive humanity. The Bible gives us no indication of any other life in this universe. Furthermore, the existence of aliens is not consistent with the order and purpose of the gospel. Christ died for humanity on Earth. We are all born into sin because of Adam (Romans 5:12). Aliens are not included in Adam's sin, nor are they included in Christ's redemption. Christians must, therefore, conclude that "aliens" are of demonic origin.

The apostle Paul wrote:

> **And I will keep on doing what I am doing in order to cut the ground from under those who want an opportunity to be considered equal with us in the things they boast about. For such men are false apostles, deceitful workmen, masquerading as apostles of Christ. And no wonder, for Satan himself masquerades as an angel of light. It is not surprising, then, if his servants masquerade as servants of righteousness. Their end will be what their actions deserve (II Corinthians 11:12-15 NIV).**

There are many who will not believe in angels because they are associated with religion. However, these same people will believe in aliens since (they believe) aliens are evolved creatures. This being their argument, they are absolved of revering any creator. Since aliens are usually identified with light and enlightenment, it follows that this scripture is not exclusive to false (or demonic) angels, but also to demonic manifestations in the form of aliens.

All in all, the alien message is one of confusion and deception. Author William Alnor points out that aliens of the '50s claimed to be from the moon, and then Mars and Venus. In the '60s and '70s when we learned that life (in any remotely human form) is absolutely impossible on the moon, Mars, and Venus, the aliens then claimed to be from farther and farther points. It is also interesting to note that they always seem to be from some point that is the farthest reach from Earth, but that point is still identified and known to humans. It is apparent that either the humans who claim to be talking with aliens are lying, or the "aliens" with whom humans are talking are lying.

The point is that these "aliens" want to distort the gospel, take attention from Jesus, or at least call into doubt the creation story of the Bible. If one will entertain a seed of doubt, then he allows his faith to become polluted and even corrupted. Our faith in Jesus is just that: faith. I do not want to oversimplify, but the fact is that man cannot know the mind of God. Man cannot comprehend the awesome creation that extends beyond his highest aspiration. To presume that this creation occurred in any manner other than the way that is affirmed by Jesus Himself is to believe a lie.

Chapter 8: Witches, Crystals, and Candles

Witches

In the 1960s, the television situation comedy *Bewitched* was a big
hit. Families would come together to share the wit and wisdom of
Samantha, the witch. Samantha was a good witch. Some of
Samantha's relatives were a bit more mischievous, but none were
truly *evil* in the classical sense. For this reason, we dismissed the
idea and watched regularly.

Today, one can watch *Sabrina, the Teenage Witch* which features
a black cat which talks to Sabrina. Sabrina is a student in high
school. She lives the lives of countless adolescents and faces the
same problems. The show *Charmed* features several active,
seductive female witches. There is also a television show, *Buffy
the Vampire Slayer,* which features gothic fare.

The New Age is full of witches. Many of these witches, like
Samantha, do not fit the classic idea of witches standing over a
steaming cauldron of some disgusting brew. These witches are
(seemingly) ordinary people. They are bankers, truck drivers,
teachers, clerical workers, and students. These people regularly
delve into seances, voodoo, and in some cases, open satanic ritual.
Some are even so bold as to openly claim Satan as their master.

Today, witchcraft masquerades as other things. You may see the
term "wicca." This is merely the arcane word for witchcraft. You
will also see references to "pagan" religion or paganism. This is
also witchcraft. Also common in witchcraft is the spelling of
magic as "magik" or "magick."

Witchcraft and gothic subcultures are becoming a particular
problem among teens and adolescents. Students are seduced by
the idea of power, especially in an age when they feel powerless
and are struggling to achieve their own independence. Other
factors calculate into the problem. Adolescents naturally want to
deviate from their parents' culture. The baby boomers all grew up
in an age when social limits were being tested and changed. I
recall countless of my friends saying that when they were adults

The Millennium Agenda

they would let their kids do whatever they wanted. I'm afraid many of them may have done exactly that.

In an age where children already have very few limits, it becomes even more dangerous for them to stretch the limits of their parents' tolerance. One of the ways they may do this is by experimenting with the gothic subculture. This subculture, while not explicitly witchcraft, shares many common ideas and can easily lead directly into overt witchcraft.

First, witchcraft and gothic culture both deal in the mystic. This is often manifested in seances or other spirit contact. Secondly, they both are concerned with death and afterlife contact. And while most kids will claim to be involved in the gothic culture because of peer identity, it will likely draw them into more sinister and satanic influences and activities.

Gothic culture is characterized by black clothing (usually plain), black hair (sometimes with a red sheen), black fingernails and lips as well as black eye shadow. This goes for both male and female. To emphasize the contrast, the skin is made up in pale shades. Any jewelry consists of skulls, bones, snakes, crosses, and swastikas. Their demeanor is somber and intentionally

The symbol at the left, the pentacle, is a common symbol for witchcraft. The five points are said to represent earth, air, fire, water and spirit. The symbol on the right, the baphomet, forms a goat's head and is the symbol of Satan.

weird. And as a final note, both male and female may wear fishnet hose.

Parents should not simply consider this a passing phase. My parents once pastored a church in rural North Texas. A family moved into the area from a metropolitan area specifically to get their daughter, who claimed to be a witch, away from the gothic subculture in the school district.   Unfortunately, rather than removing their daughter from the gothic culture, they simply brought it to the rural school. The girl wasted no time in developing a coven in the new school.

The parents tried tactics such as burning her satanic books and gothic clothing, but the girl was always able to get more, and has done so consistently. The parents are Christians, but find themselves powerless in this situation. It is clear, now, that a little prevention would have been worth more than any cure.

Author James Van Praagh is a psychic medium who channels spirits of the dead. He describes his introduction into the occult as an accident. He states that while playing with a Ouija board, he and a friend tried to conjure the spirit of Janis Joplin. After several minutes, he claims that he achieved some kind of response. He then claims that "what started out as a gag between two kids was a somewhat entertaining induction into what has become my career."[45]

In other words, he became involved in spirit contact and the occult while playing with a Ouija board. While many kids and adults may claim that their dabbling with occult items are all in innocence and for fun, they may find themselves drawn in deeper without even knowing it. This is a good example of the importance of running from even the appearance of evil.

Getting back to witches, some claim to be "good" witches, only casting "good" spells. Others are unashamed in their evil intent. Witches use sorcery, necromancy, and voodoo. **Sorcery** is the use of supernatural power over others through the assistance of spirits. It is also considered to be magic by use of spirits. **Necromancy** is the practice of supposedly communicating with the spirits of the dead in order to predict the future. This is characterized by seances and channeling. **Voodoo** is the ability to cause harm or to curse others by use of a charm. That charm is a personal effect of the target person.

The Bible is very clear on the subject of witchcraft. In fact, anyone found involved in any type of spiritism or witchcraft is to be executed! "Do not allow a sorceress to live" (Exodus 22:18 NIV). "I will set my face against the person who turns to mediums and spiritists to prostitute himself by following them, and I will cut him off from his people" (Leviticus 20:6 NIV). These commands also apply to telephone fortune-tellers, palm readers, and spirit guides.

The appendix of *UFOs in the New Age* by William M. Alnor contains a remarkable story of an individual who had been caught up in occult activity and was able to break free.

Crystals

I think that crystals fascinate everyone. They come in a variety of shapes, sizes, and colors. Some crystals, which are called fluorite, seem to glow when exposed to ultraviolet light. But all crystals have an interesting property. Applying pressure or electrical current will cause them to resonate, or vibrate. They vibrate at a constant and known rate and some are used to regulate radio signals. Chances are that your watch has a quartz crystal in it.

Timekeepers, by international agreement, define the second as 9,192,631,770 oscillations of a cesium (crystal)-controlled clock.

New Age advocates believe that crystals also provide healing and strength. They believe that the oscillations of a crystal can emulate or synchronize the "natural energy" or "healing frequency" of the human body. This all gets back to the idea of the life-force energy.

Legends and fairy tales tell of how crystals provide the holder with power. In the Disney story of Aladdin, the court wizard, Jafar, uses a crystal to control physical matter, and to divine information and such. Nearly every cartoon on Saturday morning advocates some form of crystal magic. Magazines sell crystal pendants claiming that they provide health and healing. Mystics claim to see the future in crystal balls. The use of crystals and other stones originates from alchemy. Alchemy is the ancient science that speculated that lead could be transformed into gold. This grew into the chemical sciences that we know today.

Even though crystals do vibrate under certain circumstances, the fact is the vibrations of a crystal are so minute that they can only be detected with precise electronic equipment. And, there is no evidence that any stone can provide healing or strength.

In her book *Crystal Ascension*, Catherine Bowman explains how to use crystals for healing and enlightenment. Her claims are consistent with New Age thinking that the vibrations of crystals are used to tune your natural energies for health, healing, romance, etc.

According to Bowman, all things (vegetable, animal, mineral, and including human) vibrate at varying frequencies.[46] Bowman says of healing:

> **If I generate the thought that I will get sick, I automatically draw these vibrations to my aura. If, on the other hand, I repeat affirmations that I am of a healthy body and mind, illness will not be attracted to me.**[47]

She goes on to describe aura and defines "subtle bodies" as opposed to our physical bodies:

> **Our skin is encased by approximately four inches of energy. This cocoon or force field, called the etheric body, consists of tiny fibers not unlike those found in a spider's web.**[48]

She describes two other zones: one six inches beyond the etheric called the "emotional body," and six inches beyond that, the "mental body."

She explains that placing crystals at certain chakras (power

The Millennium Agenda

centers for the body) will tune your vibrations. The first seven
chakras are as follows: the crown (on top of the head), the third
eye (forehead), throat, heart, solar plexus, spleen, and base (lower
abdomen).[49] She then describes the chakra levels: the Higher
Emotional, the Higher Mental, the Oversoul, the Master, and the
"Creator (I AM)."[50]

I found the description of the last level very interesting. She
describes the "I AM" level this way:

> **When a connection is made to this creator
> vibration, energies of our physical and
> spiritual bodies will be completely inte-
> grated into one complete being, the I Am. All
> knowledge and understanding is available
> for us to expand and express ourselves as
> beings of light.[51]**

As for using the crystals, she goes into great detail about the
different shapes and patterns of placement of the crystals. She
even demonstrates a pyramid pattern in which the individual
meditates in the center. She recommends crystals for children,
cars, and pets so that they "will develop a more congenial
disposition."[52]

She openly admits and supports the idea that "crystalology" is a
New Age practice. Crystalology is the New Age religion that
ascribes different qualities to crystals and stones. Those qualities
vary from healing to making the user more wise.

On the World Wide Web, a merchant advertises crystals for sale.
She claims to have handpicked the crystals.

> **They have never been exposed to dynamite,
> and were hand cut and polished. Therefore,
> they maintain their original, specific ener-
> gies. I hope you appreciate, respect, and use
> them only in their intended manner.[53]**

Dynamite, she believes, would destroy the natural frequency and
healing properties of the stone. She concludes:

> **In Love and Light[54]**

a typical New Age salutation.

Among her collection, she lists these items with their supposed abilities:

AMBER: Luck, Healing, & Protection
AMETHYST: Healing, Increased Psychic Ability, & Addictions
APACHE TEAR: Protection from Psychic Attack, Good Luck
HEMATITE: Centering the spirit, Healing, Grounding
OBSIDIAN: Transmutes Negative Energy into Positive Protection [55]

And so on.

The Bible tells of the use of stones. The priests wore stones on their garments to symbolize the various tribes of Israel. Jacob set large stones erect to demonstrate a contract. They did not, however, regard the stones as a source of power. Crystals and other stones are merely creations. God created them.

Our strength comes from God. Our healing comes from Jesus' suffering. All prophecy comes from the Father. We must remember that all power belongs to God and it is He who gives it to us.

Candles

Candles are often used in witchcraft. According to a book I came across, the color, shape, and scent of a candle as well as engravings carved on a candle govern its power. The book also instructed the reader on how to place different herbs on or around a candle for further powers. The individual is supposed to invoke protection, good fortune, health and such while meditating and burning the candle.

While strolling through a local mall, I happened upon a shop that specialized in "natural" things. A greater part of the store was devoted to crystalline objects, crystal fragments, polished stones, and the like. The remainder of the shop had wind chimes, hand carved trinkets, and candles. On a particular candle was a piece of paper. The paper had writing on it and I picked it up to read it:

Ritual Candles
Protection

I am fully prosont in the placc of
the Mystery wherein desire and
destiny become one...

This is only part of the inscription. This is basically a prayer—a prayer in which the individual invokes protection *from* some unknown *by* some unknown. Particular flag words are "Ritual," "Mystery" (especially since it was capitalized), "pure energy," and "universal protection." Other candles are used for various magic spells, which can include causing someone to fall in love with you, or causing harm to someone.

Chapter 9: Near Death Experiences and Afterlife Contact

Misguided by the Light?

In her book *Embraced by The Light*, Betty Eadie claims to have died, gone to heaven, and met Jesus. After talking with Him, Betty returned to life to share her experience. This type of experience is called a "Near Death Experience." It is called *near* death since it, in fact, is not final. Many New Age teachers claim to have received their doctrines from near death experiences.

Betty Eadie's book explains doctrines that she claims she received directly from Jesus Christ. She claims to be a Christian. But there is something strangely wrong with her message.

Her book goes into detail of her "death" and passage to the afterlife. A common theme among near death experiences is that of passing through a dark tunnel toward a light. At the end of the tunnel, Eadie claims to have met and talked to Jesus. She claims that, among other things, Jesus told her, "You're being too harsh on yourself "[56] as she reviewed her life and felt sorrow for her sin. She claims that the way of salvation is simply to love each other. As she stood in front of a "council of men," she realized that "love is really the only thing that matters. Love is really the only thing that matters and love is *joy!*"[57] (emphasis hers). The closest she comes to describing a salvation experience is in the following:

> **Of all knowledge, however, there is none more essential than knowing Jesus Christ. I was told that he is the door through which we will all return. He is the only door through [which] we can return. Whether we learn of Jesus Christ here or while in the spirit, we must eventually accept him and surrender to his love.**[58]

Her phrase "here or while in the spirit'" means that we will learn and trust in Jesus either *here in this lifetime,* or *in the spirit world after death.* She consistently uses the word "spirit" to indicate afterlife beings.

The Millennium Agenda

Further, she adds that all religions are necessary because different people have different spiritual understanding. In other words, all roads lead to heaven.

> **Each of us, I was told, is at a different level of spiritual development and understanding. Each person is therefore prepared for a different level of spiritual knowledge. All religions upon the earth are necessary because there are people who need what they teach. People in one religion may not have a complete understanding of the Lord's gospel and never will have while in that religion. But that religion is used as a stepping stone to further knowledge. Each church fulfills spiritual needs that perhaps others cannot fill.**[59]

This information, she purports, was given to her directly by Jesus. I find it difficult to believe that Jesus would have said this since in the flesh, He declared that *He* was the only way to salvation.

And on it goes. While before the council of men, Eadie claims she was shown the events in the Garden of Eden in which she states that Eve deliberately sought to sin because she wanted to be a mother:

> **I was shown that Eve did not "fall" to temptation as much as she made a conscious decision to bring about conditions necessary for her progression**[60]

The word "progression" here can be considered a New Age buzzword analogous to "ascension." Some people claim that Lucifer was an alien who, rather than tempting Eve to sin, invited her to act in order to accelerate her progression. Mythology about Lilith (the first wife of Adam, according to Hebrew mysticism) also claims that Eve consciously transgressed in order to become enlightened.

Eadie states that each individual chooses—before birth—the

illness or manner in which they will die. She brings up an illustration of an alcoholic who chose that position in life in order to remind another person (in particular) to be kind to the less fortunate. Reading between the lines of this philosophy implies that we should not try to rehabilitate that alcoholic since his role is vital to the overall plan. It removes the obligation of the individual to his fellow man. And, as earlier quoted, she implies that all humanity will someday acknowledge and trust Jesus either "here or while in the spirit." This also relieves each individual of his or her duty to witness.

Eadie states that to her surprise, she learned that "Jesus was a separate being from God with his own divine purpose and I knew that God was our mutual Father."[61] This, she explains, is in contrast to Jesus being one and the same as God.

Eadie claims that "the spirit by spirit prodigies"[62] provided many of our inventions and innovations. This sounds like spirit contact. Friedrich August Kekule (1829-1896), a famous organic chemist, claimed to have conceived of the molecular structure of the benzene molecule while in a dozed state. According to Eadie, this vision would have been given to him by spirit prodigies. The fact that Kekule's vision was that of a snake swallowing its tail is even more peculiar, since that is a common occult symbol.

Later Eadie states that "it is important for us to acquire knowledge of the spirit while we are in the flesh. The more knowledge we acquire here, the further and faster we will progress there....Some [spirits] who die as atheists...find it difficult to move on, and they become earthbound."[63]

She states that she learned that "sin is not our true nature."[64] She describes prayer as beams of light ascending into heaven and the angels attend to the brightest lights (most sincere prayers) first and then the others in turn.

In the midst of all of Eadie's philosophies and doctrines that she claims to have received from either Jesus Himself or other guides are statements such as the following:

Under the guidance of the Savior I learned

> **that it was important for me to accept all experience as potentially good. I needed to accept my purpose and station in life. I could take the negative things that had happened to me and try to overcome their effects. I could forgive my enemies, even love them, and thereby nullify any bad influence they may have had on me.**[65]

This is consistent with:

> **And we know that in all things God works for the good of those who love him, who have been called according to his purpose (Romans 8:28 NIV).**

And with:

> **But I tell you: Love your enemies and pray for those who persecute you (Matthew 5:44 NIV).**

However, the problem with her statement is not so much what she says, but with what she does *not* say. She never mentions Jesus' blood buying our healing (Isaiah 53:5), the necessity of His death to redeem our sins (Hebrews 2:14), or the relevance of His resurrection (Acts 2:24).

I could probably forgive the errors in Betty Eadie's book as syntactical preference, if it were not for the prolific use of New Age idioms and buzzwords. With this in mind, Betty Eadie's message (although it sounds very Christian) is *highly* consistent with New Age philosophy and *highly* contradictory to the gospel— even though she claims throughout the book to be Christian.

First, God is acutely concerned with our sin. It is sin that keeps us separated from Him. In fact, God sent His son to die because of our sin (Romans 3:25), so that we could commune with Him. Secondly, Jesus said that everyone *must* confess Him as Lord to be saved (Matthew 10:32). And thirdly, all roads do not lead to heaven. Jesus stated with no reservation: "I am the way" (John 14:6).

Near Death Experiences and Afterlife Contact

We must actually consider the nature of Eadie's experience. Was it really a near death experience? Doug Groothius, in his book *Deceived by the Light*, explains that Eadie was in the hospital for a hysterectomy. She was not in the operating room or even in intensive care when she supposedly "died." Her hospital records do not even record any incident on the date that she claims to have had this experience.[66]

So, it seems clear to me that Betty Eadie did not really talk to Jesus. In fact, Jesus Himself stated:

> **No one has ever gone into heaven except the one who came from heaven—the Son of Man (John 3:13 NIV).**

This verse is not stating that no one ever went to heaven, but rather that no one who has gone to heaven has ever come to earth to tell about it except Jesus himself.

Channeling

James Van Praagh, the professional psychic medium mentioned in Chapter 8, explains the afterlife in his book *Talking To Heaven*.* He claims to channel spirits of the dead and animals (pets) as well.[67] He records several channeling experiences in the book, which convey bits of information regarding the afterlife such as the following:

> **An unexpected spirit usually emerges toward the end of a session. It is comforting to know that even on the other side manners are meaningful. An unexpected spirit will wait until a sitter has reunited with a loved one or until an appropriate opportunity. Frequently, it is the unexpected spirit who has the most compelling message to share with the sitter.[68]**

The "sitter" is the person paying for the channeling session. I

---

* From *Talking To Heaven* by James Van Praagh, copyright ©1997 by James Van Praagh. Used by permission of Dutton, a division of Penguin Putnam, Inc.

The Millennium Agenda

found this passage somewhat humorous, albeit absurd.

Praagh, like Eadie, also says that individuals choose their method of death before they come into this life.[69] But then, oddly, he states that to commit suicide is a "terrible mistake."[70] If we choose our method of death, then our death is predestined. How, then, can committing suicide be a mistake if it is predestined? He does not resolve this paradox.

In one part of his philosophy, he mixes references to Karma *and* God:

> **All our actions are repaid in kind, positively or negatively, in this life or another lifetime. The law of cause and effect is a natural, immutable law of the universe, and there is a resolution to every experience by way of Karmic action or the grace of God.**[71]

The belief in Karma and reincarnation, as defined by the Hindu, is mutually exclusive with "God." For Mr. Praagh to mix the references is a strong indication of his New Age influence which allows mixing of religious ideas. This is consistent with his idea of creation in which "*All* things are created from universal thought" (emphasis his). "Universal Thought"[72] is a concept analogous to Cosmic Consciousness or Harmonic Convergence, in which all beings capable of thought concentrate their thought in a certain aspect to bring about some desired result. Further emphasizing this point, he states that everyone is "part of the universal energy of God."[73] Another New Age concept is that God is energy and all people are mere extensions of that energy. This is actually a distortion of the Hindu concept of the Brahman in which people are like solar flares that pull away from and emerge back into the collective energy or life force. He also makes reference to "creative force within ourselves," alluding to the idea of Universal Thought.

He denies the status of the Israelites as a "chosen" people, thus allowing for an anti-Semitic attitude. As far as salvation, Praagh claims that "when we pass on to the other side, the only question we will be asked has to do with the *amount of love* we have in our

Near Death Experiences and Afterlife Contact

hearts"[74] (emphasis his).

Another channeler utilizes automatic writing in his sessions. In automatic writing the medium enters a trance state or some other channeling state, and receives messages that are written by his hand but not from his volition. Some of psychic George Anderson's sessions are recorded in a book by Joel Martin* and Patricia Romanowski titled *We Don't Die: George Anderson's Conversations With The Other Side*. In this book, we are witness to one of the channeling sessions and introduced to George Anderson:

> **George wasn't what she was expecting. He was slightly built, with curly black hair and neatly trimmed beard....George said a prayer, asking God for protection and crossed himself.**[75]

It is apparent that Mr. Anderson was from a Catholic background—having "crossed" himself after a prayer. However, I must interject at this point. We are strictly commanded to avoid spirit contact, and those who contact spirits.

> **Do not turn to mediums or seek out spiritists, for you will be defiled by them. I am the LORD your God (Leviticus 19:31 NIV).**

During one channeling session, Mr. Anderson channeled a young man named David who had recently been killed in an accident. The mother was paying for the sitting. Mr. Anderson encountered a spirit identifying itself as the woman's son as well as a second spirit identifying itself as a young woman from the same neighborhood who had been killed several months earlier.

> **George returned to the young girl who had passed over before David. "He keeps saying, 'she met me when I came over.'"**

The Millennium Agenda

> "Yes." [the mother]
>
> "'She brought me into the light,' He says."[76]

Mr. Anderson continues:

> George paused and looked up from his writing and continued, "He's in good hands. He keeps assuring you that. And the prayers that you've been sending help tremendously. He says, 'I'm in the light. I'm in the light.' "[77]

Yet another reference to the "light." There is not a lot of description of the "light" here; however, it is an interesting parallel. Speaking of prayer for the dead:

> George stopped writing now. "He says 'keep the prayers coming very quick.' He says, 'Don't worry about me. All is well with me. I'm in good hands.' Undoubtedly, you've been praying for your son. He says please not to stop. Keep it coming. He's in the light because of it. It means he's with God, so to speak."[78]

The phrase "with God, so to speak" is somewhat humorous to me. God is so absolute, that He could never be referenced with "so to speak." To speak of God in so transient of terms reduces the magnificence of God. On the other hand, the phrase gives a much clearer picture of how Mr. Anderson sees God—not as an omniscient, omnipresent, immutable, loving being, but rather as some essence of energy. Mr. Anderson's concept of God is consistent with the New Age concept of God being merely a light into which we enter when we die.

We also see in this account that the deceased was not faced with any judgment for his actions during his lifetime. There is no mention of Jesus, and we are left with the sense that all spirits enter "heaven" or the light. In the New Age, heaven is just a light, or energy, which is love.

Among all the writings that I have encountered, I am overwhelmed with the emphasis on "love." Not that love is a bad thing. Jesus advocated love—even to the extent of loving one's enemies. But when the emphasis on love eclipses Jesus' act of sacrifice and salvation, then that love becomes an evil thing.

Jesus compared the love that one should have for Him and His kingdom in the following manner.

> **If anyone comes to me and does not hate his father and mother, his wife and children, his brothers and sisters—yes, even his own life— he cannot be my disciple (Luke 14:26 NIV).**

Jesus is not saying that we should literally "hate" our families (whom we love more than any other people on earth), but that our love for our families, *compared to* our love for Him, would be the difference between love and hate. In other words, the magnitude of love for our families compared to those we hate should be equal in magnitude to the love we feel for Him compared to the love we have for our family.

We can summarize then that while love is important, our love for Jesus should be absolutely paramount over any other love we feel.

It is obvious that these philosophies of the afterlife and methods of salvation are spurious. This being the case, from whom, then, do people get these false doctrines? Satan masquerades as an angel of light, looking for someone to deceive. Satan wants to deceive all believers and anyone who would believe. If he is able to shift our focus from Jesus, then he has succeeded. And what better way to deceive people than to give them a target which is close, very close to Christian doctrine, but just enough off to cause the destruction of mankind. In fact, by masquerading as the truth, it is essential for him to actually appear to be truth, good, and desirable. In so doing, he tempts us to shift our focus from Jesus as our salvation to "love" as our salvation.

Be aware of people who claim to have received messages from Jesus, or an angel. That message *must be consistent with the gospel.* If it is not consistent with the gospel, then consider it a false doctrine and flee from it!

> **Dear friends, do not believe every spirit, but**

> **test the spirits to see whether they are from God, because many false prophets have gone out into the world (I John 4:1 NIV).**

The Gospel of Luke records the account of Jesus' story of Lazarus, the beggar, and the rich man. Since Lazarus is named specifically, this is believed to be a true story, and not just an allegory. In the story, Lazarus had begged at the gate of the rich man's house and the rich man considered him unworthy of his pity. After they both die, the rich man finds himself in hell begging Abraham for mercy. He asks first for Lazarus, who is now with Abraham, to dip his finger in water and moisten his tongue.

Abraham explains that even if it was allowable, it would be impossible because of the great chasm fixed between them. The rich man continues:

> **He answered, "Then I beg you, father, send Lazarus to my father's house, for I have five brothers. Let him warn them, so that they will not also come to this place of torment."**
>
> **Abraham replied, "They have Moses and the Prophets; let them listen to them."**
>
> **"No, father Abraham," he said, "but if some- one from the dead goes to them, they will repent."**
>
> **He said to him, "If they do not listen to Moses and the Prophets, they will not be convinced even if someone rises from the dead" (Luke 16:27-31 NIV).**

In this account Jesus Himself proclaims that there will not be prophetic messages from the afterlife. We are given the prophets, and the teachings of Jesus Himself. If we do not believe them, then we will not believe someone with messages from the afterlife.

Section III

False Prophets
and
The Fading Christ

The Millennium Agenda

Chapter 10: Doubting Thomas

A recent newspaper article begins:

> **Dallas—"What kind of God does the world
> need now?"**
>
> **This is a peculiar question. If God *is*, then
> the only possible answer is "the real one."
> But *if* God is, the more important question is
> "What kind of world does *God* need now?"**
>
> **I take it, however, that the question con-
> cerns the *truth* about God. Does God exist?
> If so, how could we ever know unless God
> revealed Himself? Has God revealed Him-
> self? And has this revelation any abiding
> significance?**[79]

I was intrigued by these words found in the Religion section of a
secular publication. Of course, I find the answer to the questions
above in the person of Jesus. However, many look at Jesus, and
still have questions.

One of Satan's tactics against the gospel is the interjection of
doubt.

> **Now the serpent was more crafty than any of
> the wild animals the LORD God had made.
> He said to the woman, "Did God really say,
> 'You must not eat from any tree in the gar-
> den'?" (Genesis 3:1 NIV).**

The fact is that the man and woman were commanded to not eat
of only one tree. In fact, when the woman answers, she adds to
the law:

> **But God did say, "You must not eat fruit
> from the tree that is in the middle of the
> garden, and you must not touch it, or you
> will die" (Genesis 3:3 NIV).**

The law was not to eat the fruit of the tree. Nothing was said
about touching the tree.

It is unfortunate that people seem eager to explore doubt rather than stand on the faith of the gospel. As Christians, we believe that:

> **All Scripture is God-breathed and is useful for teaching, rebuking, correcting and training in righteousness, so that the man of God may be thoroughly equipped for every good work (II Timothy 3:16-17 NIV).**

We believe that all scripture is divinely inspired. In fact, the Old Testament, or Torah, is the historical record preserved by the patriarchs. The early Christian Church assembled the New Testament. It was assembled from various writings that were available at the time. *The Concise Columbia Encyclopedia* explains:

> **Selection of New Testament books as canonical was slow, the present canon appearing for the first time in the Festal Epistle of St. Athanasius (A.D. 367).**[80]

Again, we believe that the hearts and hands of the Church leaders selected the appropriate text to include and exclude. This process was more than just pulling together all available documentation. In fact, there were numerous documents that were examined. There had been many sects and cults that had perverted the gospel with ritual sexual immorality and forms of paganism.

The Church leaders were intent on assembling a unified canon of scripture that correctly represented the historical record of Jesus and His teachings. The teachings that they selected were those which conveyed the historical life of Jesus: The four Gospels, and the apostolic letters. The four Gospels strongly corroborate each other and thus provide a solid foundation for the historical life and teachings of Jesus. The apostolic letters are included since they convey the Christian faith directly from the apostles, having received the gospel from Jesus Himself. *The Concise Columbia Encyclopedia* continues:

> **The greatest English translation (and one of**

The Millennium Agenda

the most influential English prose works) is the Authorized Version (AV), or King James Version (KJV), of 1611, made by a group of churchmen and scholars led by Lancelot Andrewes.[81]

Still, men and women who claim to be Christian scholars interject doubt into the gospel. The fact is that many modern scholars simply do not believe that the Bible is the infallible word of God. They believe various levels of truth. There are some that believe that the Old Testament contains errors and legend, but still is just as useful for guidance. Some believe that the Old Testament was completely created by the Hebrews in captivity several centuries before Jesus.

Lance Wilcox, writing an article for *Bible Review,* suggests that the book of Jonah was not even intended to be scriptural, but rather a play.

For a long time, I wanted to write a play about the comic, contentious, absurd, salvific relationship between God and us—to present a comic Everyman (sic) locked in mortal (salvific) combat with Yahweh.[82]

He continues that he found this comedy in the book of Jonah as read from the *Oxford Study Edition of the New English Bible*:

The introduction suggested the story was a satire, an attack on a Jewish purity movement, represented in part by Ezra and Nehemiah.[83]

Some scholars believe that the New Testament was assembled from embellished tales of a Christ whom many wanted to see. Ironically, they preach and believe in Jesus, but somehow don't believe the entire gospel to be truth—especially the resurrection of Christ.

While Michael Baigent was researching the Priori de Sion for his book *Holy Blood, Holy Grail,* a retired Anglican priest wrote to him claiming to have:

...."incontrovertible proof" that the Crucifix-

**ion was a fraud and that Jesus was alive as
late as A.D. 45.**[84]

I wondered how anyone could not believe in Jesus' crucifixion but
still remain a Christian. The idea seemed an oxymoron. I found
the answer to this question later in Baigent's book. He cites an
"apostolic letter" of Pope John XXIII. This letter was on the
subject of "The Precious Blood of Jesus."

> **It ascribed a hitherto unprecedented signifi-
> cance to that blood. It emphasized Jesus'
> suffering as a human being and maintained
> that the redemption of mankind had been
> affected by the shedding of his blood. In the
> context of Pope John's letter, Jesus' human
> Passion and the shedding of his blood as-
> sume a greater consequence than the Resur-
> rection or even than the mechanics of the
> Crucifixion.**[85]

This statement allows one to deny the death and resurrection of
Jesus and remain a Christian. The Pope's statement is that the
suffereing of Jesus was sufficient to purchase our salvation—that
His death was unnecessary. The idea is outrageous. The entire
idea of a savior is that our debt is paid. Recall that Adam and
Eve's penalty was death—a blood debt was required. However,
God allowed for a sacrifice, a substitute. In fact, all people had to
exercise the law of sacrifice. This only paid their blood debt
temporarily. Jesus came as our ultimate blood sacrifice that
allowed us to be free of the law of sacrifice. This, then, obligates
us to worship and believe in Him and His resurrection.

> **But if it is preached that Christ has been
> raised from the dead, how can some of you
> say that there is no resurrection of the dead?
> If there is no resurrection of the dead, then
> not even Christ has been raised. And if
> Christ has not been raised, our preaching is
> useless and so is your faith...**

> **For if the dead are not raised, then Christ
> has not been raised either. And if Christ has
> not been raised, your faith is futile; you are**

> still in your sins. Then those also who have
> [died] in Christ are lost. If only for this life
> we have hope in Christ, we are to be pitied
> more than all men (I Corinthians 15:12-14,
> 16-19 NIV).

In his letter to the Corinthians, Paul wondered how the
Corinthian church could believe in the resurrection of Jesus and
not believe in the resurrection of believers. He argues that to
deny the truth of resurrection of anyone is to deny the
resurrection of Jesus. And if Jesus was not resurrected, then
what are we talking about? Without believing in the resurrection
of Jesus, there is no salvation. For our salvation is fulfilled by His
resurrection. If He was not raised, then whom do we worship, a
deceased Lord?

This is foolishness. And Paul said that if this is our belief, then
we are more pitiful than anyone can imagine.

Likewise, if Jesus was not divine, then He could not be an
acceptable substitute for our blood debt.

An Episcopal bishop exhibits great doubt in his Christianity.
However, rather than renounce his Christianity, he advocates
changing it.

> Jesus' virgin birth assumed a view of repro-
> duction where the whole life was contained
> in the male seed. The 1724 discovery of egg
> cells rendered the virgin birth stories mean-
> ingless.
>
> ...
>
> After Charles Darwin in 1859 it became
> impossible to think of human beings as
> fallen creatures destined for hell without
> God's intervention.
>
> ...
>
> Religion based on human sacrifice has little

appeal.

...

> **So Jesus can no longer be viewed as a sacri-
> fice for sin but as the source of infinite life-
> giving love.**[86]

Bishop Spong, who is a leader in a Christian (Episcopal) Church, is telling his congregation, and the world, that Christianity is wrong—that the accounts of Jesus' virgin birth, life, and death on the cross are no longer meaningful to today's world. I am strongly convinced that this man has never known the saving grace of Jesus. I cannot understand how one can be a Christian without a Christ. Christ, in the person of Jesus, came to bring us life through His death. This very act makes Him our Christ. To deny Him that attribute, is to deny Christianity.

Nonetheless, Spong's comments about the inaccuracies of the Bible are not uncommon. Author Josh McDowell has spent many years examining the authenticity and reliability of the New Testament. The common proposal that the New Testament is based on fiction was an idea put forth by F. C. Bauer. In Josh McDowell's book *More Than A Carpenter*, he explains:

> **German critic F. C. Bauer assumed that most
> of the New Testament Scriptures were not
> written until late in the second century A.D.
> He concluded that these writings came
> basically from myths or legends that had
> developed during the lengthy interval be-
> tween the lifetime of Jesus and the time
> these accounts were set down in writing.**[87]

McDowell continues...

> **By the twentieth century, however, archaeo-
> logical discoveries had confirmed the accu-
> racy of the New Testament manuscripts.
> Discoveries of early papyri manuscripts (the
> John Ryland manuscript, A.D 130; the
> Chester Beatty Papyri, A.D. 155; and the
> Bodmer Papyri II, A.D. 200) bridged the gap**

The Millennium Agenda

<blockquote>

between the time of Christ and existing Manuscripts from a later date.[88]

</blockquote>

The Dead Sea scrolls also profoundly corroborate the gospel story.

As I have discussed earlier in Chapter 2, some archaeologists are very sensitive about examining archaeological finds in light of biblical scripture. They claim that entering a field (of study) with the preconceptions of religion will only serve to prove the preconceived desires of the explorer. This, they claim, causes the explorer to forego objectivity in his research.

However true this may be, some archaeologists seem to have taken an extreme, and in fact, anti-biblical bias in their research. In other words, they seem determined to prove that a find *is not* related to the Bible, rather than examine it objectively.

In the example given in Chapter 2, an inscription was found in the city of Dan which most readily translated "House of David." Most Christians would immediately recognize this as the dynasty of the King David of the Old Testament. Several archaeologists strongly objected to this conclusion simply because it was a "preconceived" notion. They were not, however, able to provide any reasonable alternative meaning. Other archaeologists are quick to remind us that we should not jump to conclusions about linking the inscription to the biblical David. Perhaps, but if the shoe fits…

The Sacrificial Altar at the city of Dan is represented by an aluminum frame. The original altar is no longer there because stones of any quality would have been pillaged and used for other structures.

All this talk about avoiding religious identities in archaeological research has me a bit perplexed. In our day, religion is pretty much separate from work, government, and recreation. However, in the past, especially the ancient past, religion was integral with these. For this reason, it is *necessary* to consider all archaeological evidence in light of *some* religion.

Since this is the case, then would it not be reasonable to consider the evidence in light of the prevailing religion of the region and time being examined?

Josh McDowell asserts that the gospel record is very sound when measured by United States legal requirements for documented authenticity. In his book *Evidence that Demands a Verdict*, McDowell, rather than expound on other authors, gives quote after quote from other sources regarding the validity of the New Testament. He explains that there are more than 5,300 known Greek manuscripts, over 10,000 Latin Vulgate manuscripts and at least 9,300 other early manuscripts. There are also more than 24,000 manuscript copies of portions of the New Testament that we know of.[89] By contrast, the *Iliad* by Homer has only 643 manuscripts that we know of.[90] The *Iliad* is second to the New Testament for the known number of manuscripts.

And as far as translation is concerned, there are only about 40 lines in the New Testament that are in question.[91] Considering that the New Testament contains 20,000 lines, this is a remarkable reliability.

McDowell quotes renowned Jewish archaeologist Nelson Glueck who stated that no archaeological discovery has ever controverted a biblical reference—even though some would try to indicate so. Why would so many archaeologists and other scientists be so intent on denying the historicity of the Bible? McDowell continues by pointing out that because many scientists, archaeologists, and theologians cannot accept the supernatural, they will search for or even create natural explanations for archaeological discoveries—even when those discoveries point to a supernatural cause.[92]

A Deception in Miracles

A study guide was published several years ago titled *A Course in Miracles*. This "course" is of interesting origin. Its author, or "scribe" as she refers to herself, is Dr. Helen Schucman. Dr. Schucman claims that a voice speaking to her, which identified

The Millennium Agenda

itself as Jesus, is the author of the material. She claims that Jesus is speaking to her "to correct some misconceptions we have had about what he taught and what he did on earth."[93]

The *Course* has three volumes. The first is the text of the course, the second is a workbook for students, and the third is a manual for teachers.

When asked why this *Course* was created, Dr. Schucman replied:

> **The world's situation is worsening to an alarming degree. People all over the world are being called on to help and are making their individual contributions as part of an overall pre-arranged plan.**
>
> **Because of an acute emergency however, the usual slow, evolutionary process is being by-passed by what might be described as a "Celestial-Speed-Up."[94]**

A follower of the *Course*, Robert Perry published his own Internet site explaining some of the *Course's* thought system. Of particular interest were these two points:

> **We have lost touch with reality and so need the Holy Spirit's help to be restored to sanity.**
>
> **God created an extension of Himself, the Holy Spirit, and sent Him into our dreaming minds to heal their nightmares. He is the bridge of return, ... Jesus is the manifestation of the Holy Spirit. He is both [sic] our model, the pattern that we follow, and an inner teacher, an extension of the Holy Spirit in our minds.**
>
> **His Message is that we never sinned, never changed ourselves. We need only change our minds.**

> The message of the Holy Spirit is that the
> separation never occurred. We never did the
> horrible crime we think we did....It only
> happened in our dreams. Therefore, Heaven
> is still our home and the Love of God is still
> our sacred right. To claim this right we
> need not change the world, purify or perfect
> our souls, please or appease God, make
> virtuous sacrifices, nor pay for our sins. We
> don't need to *do* anything, only undo, only
> clear away the blocks to knowing what is
> already true.[95]

Let's look at the first point above. From the Gospel accounts, Jesus came to man first, and *afterward came* the manifestation of the Holy Spirit.

> But I tell you the truth: It is for your good
> that I am going away. Unless I go away, the
> Counselor will not come to you; but if I go, I
> will send him to you (John 16:7 NIV).

> But the Counselor, the Holy Spirit, whom the
> Father will send in my name, will teach you
> all things and will remind you of everything
> I have said to you (John 14:26 NIV).

In these passages, Jesus, the teacher, tells us that the comforter, the Holy Spirit, will be given to us only after He leaves us. This indicates that the advent of the Holy Spirit is an act subsequent to that of Jesus' death. Further, we know that Jesus was present at the creation of the world.

> In the beginning was the Word, and the
> Word was with God, and the Word was God.

> He was with God in the beginning. Through
> him all things were made; without him
> nothing was made that has been made.

> In him was life, and that life was the light of
> men. The light shines in the darkness, but
> the darkness has not understood it (John

The Millennium Agenda

1:1-5 NIV).

The "Word" in the above passage is commonly agreed to be a reference to the preincarnate Jesus. Jesus was the Light that was the "Light of Men." This, then, leads us to conclude that Jesus is part and parcel with God and thus preceded the advent, or at least the presence, of the Holy Spirit with men.

Now let's look at Perry's second point above. This point seems to go the extra mile in stating that man is not separated from God and thus does not need redemption. Quite the opposite, it states that man has the *right* to be with God. Contrast this with what the Bible says.

> **For all have sinned and fall short of the glory of God (Romans 3:23 NIV).**

I find it hard to get around the "all" word. If this is the case, then we *do* have a debt to pay. In Old Testament times, a law was put forward for people to present themselves to God. In fact, the closest that they could come was to the outer area of the temple. The priests alone were allowed to enter the inner parts, and only the High Priest was allowed to enter into the Holy of Holies. He wore bells on his clothing and a rope on his leg. If he was not pure when he entered the Holy of Holies, he would die (the bells would go silent) and would be dragged out by the rope.

But did this law fulfill the debt that man had to pay for his sins? Paul, in his letter to the Romans, says "no." In fact, it is only through faith in Jesus that we are redeemed.

> **But now a righteousness from God, apart from law, has been made known, to which the Law and the Prophets testify. This righteousness from God comes through faith in Jesus Christ to all who believe. There is no difference (Romans 3:21–22).**

And all those who sinned:

> **...are justified freely by his grace through the redemption that came by Christ Jesus (Romans 3:24 NIV).**

Salvation came by *grace* by way of Jesus Christ. If, then, it is by grace, then salvation is not a right, but a privilege.

In the third volume of the *Course*, Dr. Schucman describes a teacher. A teacher of God, she says, is anyone who decides to be one. In fact, this person need not even believe in God to be a teacher of God:

> **He has entered an agreement with God even if he does not yet believe in Him. He [the teacher] has become a bringer of salvation.**[96]

She claims that sickness is a choice of the afflicted and that we bring illness upon ourselves in order to learn some lesson.

> **Healing is accomplished the instant the sufferer no longer sees any value in pain. Who would choose suffering unless he thought it brought him something, and something of value to him?**[97]

As far as the role of Jesus, Shucman says, "The term sacrifice is altogether meaningless."[98] She also states, "The way to salvation can be found by those who believe in reincarnation and by those who do not."[99] And finally, to call upon the name of Jesus:

> **Is this merely an appeal to magic? A name does not heal, nor does an invocation call forth any special power.**[100]

Jesus tells us in the Bible:

> **And I will do whatever you ask *in my name*, so that the Son may bring glory to the Father. You may ask me for anything *in my name*, and I will do it (John 14:13-14 NIV).**

One day as Peter and John were about to enter the temple, they saw a crippled man begging for alms. At this Peter said:

> **Silver or gold I do not have, but what I have I give you. In the name of Jesus Christ of Nazareth, walk (Acts 3:6 NIV).**

Peter helped the man to his feet. The man stood and began to jump and praise God. The crowd who had gathered by now was

The Millennium Agenda

astonished. Peter addressed the crowd:

> **By faith *in the name of Jesus*, this man whom you see and know was made strong. It is *Jesus' name* and the faith that comes through him that has given this complete healing to him, as you can all see (Acts 3:16 NIV).**

The Celestine Propaganda

In the book titled *The Celestine Prophecy* by James Redfield, the reader is taken on a journey to Peru where the main character searches for the "insights" to a happy life. The story reveals nine of these "insights." The main character must battle the elements, the jungle, governmental agencies, and the Christian Church establishment—all who want to prevent these insights from becoming public.

The story is cataloged as fiction, but is told as truth. According to the story, the insights are recorded on ancient manuscripts and the aforementioned agencies want them to remain concealed to maintain their own "monopoly" on the secrets to a happy life. The premise is that if the "real" secrets were to become public, then there would be no need for the organized church—Christian or otherwise.

Redfield revealed in a book titled *The Celestine Vision* that his intention for *The Celestine Prophecy* and a follow-up book to it was not to create a fascinating thriller novel, but rather to impart philosophical (and indeed, religious) tenets. He refers to his books as "adventure parables."

> **They were my way of illustrating what I believe is a new spiritual awareness sweeping humanity. I was trying to describe the personal revelations that each of us seems to be experiencing as our awareness increases.**[101]

Because of the general appeal of his tenets—and their end result—people buy into the philosophy.

In short, he teaches a variation of Hinduism. The universe, he claims, is intelligent and "built to respond to our consciousness."[102] He advocates "synchronicity," which is a concept developed by Carl Jung to try to explain the uncanny string of coincidences that fall in our path. Synchronicity, according to Jung, is the universe's intelligence coordinating events on your behalf.

He concludes that there is no hell nor "fallen angels." These, he claims, are simply "metaphors for the pitfalls inherent in human evolution."[103]

Redfield defines god as "the creative force behind the human condition."[104] The purpose of prayer, he claims, is to "lead to an inner transformative experience, where our connection to the divine is perceived in an ecstatic manner of being one with the whole universe."[105]

He uses terms like "godhead" and "universal one-ness" which are terms that have meaning in the Hindu aspect of the Brahman (everything congealed into a single mass). He, like Betty Eadie (*Embraced by the Light*), claims that all religions lead to heaven. And since there is no hell, then there is no incentive to evangelize (except, of course, to their way of thinking).

Jesus in the Age of Aquarius

I ran across a book called *The Aquarian Gospel of Jesus the Christ*. The author was listed simply as "Levi." This book was, in fact, written by Levi H. Dowling (1844-1911) and is copyrighted by Eva S. Dowling and Leo W. Dowling (1907).

This book is written in what sounds like King James English (the *King James Version* of the Bible was transcribed circa 1644). It represents itself as biblical and factual. The fact is that Levi Dowling wrote the book in the late 19th and early 20th centuries and claims that it is a clarification of the life of Jesus.

Mr. Dowling, however, makes no mention of the virgin birth and goes on to explain away the physical resurrection of Jesus.

The Millennium Agenda

> **And Pilate sent his scribe who placed upon the stone the seal of Rome, in such a way that he who moved the stone would break the seal. To break the Roman seal meant death to him who broke the seal (Section XX; Resh 172:4–5).**[106]

> **Then they returned; the stone was in its place; the seal was not disturbed, and they resumed their watch. Now, Jesus did not sleep within the tomb. The body is the manifest of soul; but soul is soul without manifest. And in the realm of souls, unmanifest, the Lord went forth and taught (Section XX; Resh 172:14-16).**[107]

As you can perhaps see, Mr. Dowling wrote his book in chapter/verse form. Interestingly, the *King James Version* of the Bible was set in this form because when it was written, neither the original texts nor King James' English utilized punctuation marks. For Mr. Dowling to write in this fashion clearly indicates that he wanted his book to be perceived as authentic biblical text when it is not.

He claims that Jesus "was made perfect through suffering; for this is the only way to perfection."[108] Further, he claims that Jesus was not always the Christ:

> **Lincoln was not always President, and Jesus was not always Christ.**[109]

Within the book, Mr. Dowling describes an account (which is not recorded in any of the biblical gospels) about Jesus, where Jesus explains to a woman why her husband refused to participate in her religion:

> **Intolerance is ignorance matured.**[110]

These words are attributed to Jesus. Religious "tolerance" is a main tenet of the New Age.

I have trouble believing that this book is either divinely inspired or even fact based.

The Lost Episodes

Another book titled *The Lost Books of the Bible*[111] (various and anonymous authors) contains many ridiculous accounts attributed to Jesus. The book claims that water that had been used to wash the infant Jesus would instantly heal anyone who came in contact with it. On another account, Joseph was commissioned to build a wooden throne for the King. Having finished the throne, Joseph discovered that it was narrower than the specified width. At this, Jesus commanded His father to pull on one side and Jesus pulled on the other, miraculously widening the throne.

Again, this book is written in King James English and chapter/verse format, and even though several passages read very similar to the biblical Gospels, I am compelled to believe that it is not authentic.

Chapter 11: Priestess of Isis

Helena Blavatsky

Helena Petrovna Blavatsky was born in 1831 in the Russian Ukraine. Her mother was a novelist, her grandmother a princess of Dolgorukov (going back to the Grand Duke Rurik, founder of what became the Russian Empire). Her grandfather was a governor and she lived in a household of fifty servants.

She was baptized two days after her birth by the Russian Orthodox church in the family mansion. She lived in many mansions during her life and was always attended by a staff of servants. During her young life, Blavatsky encountered many occult practices. Although baptized into the Christian church (Russian Orthodox), she had little respect for it. She recognized the futility of baptism as the act of salvation.* This disdain may have been the catalyst for her search for other religious truth.

She claims to have encountered an "Indian" man who directed her religious activities throughout her lifetime. This man appeared to her in apparitions several times until she saw him in the flesh in England in 1851 at the Great Exhibition.

Her maternal grandfather was a political figure and served as governor or in some other governmental capacity throughout most of her early life. For this reason, she lived in mansions

Ouroboros: The serpent swallowing its tail is used by many occult groups to symbolize eternity. The symbol also forms a circle which represents the sun as a diety. This figure appeared on the cover of Helena Blavatsky's book, *The Secret Doctrine*.

---

* Most Protestant religions observe baptism as a symbol of our salvation rather than an execution of our salvation. Catholic and orthodox religions see baptism as the literal act of salvation.

provided by the state. She makes reference to the family gallery where portraits were hung. One in particular was hung so high that she had to stack several pieces of furniture on top of a table just to reach it.

Having once lived in a home that her family actually had to pay for, she complained that the rooms were like closets. Judging by the description of her lifestyle before this, I can imagine that to her, the rooms of this house were, indeed, about the size of a closet, but probably still grand by the average person's perspective. I suppose it is relative to the opulence to which she had become accustomed.

Because of her disposition, her governess told her that she would be unable to persuade a man to marry her. In fact, she said that Helena could not even get Nikifor Blavatsky, a man she despised and mocked, to marry her. Out of spite, Helena convinced the old man to marry her within three days.

She was married at the age of eighteen in 1849. She remained married only three months before she ran away and began more than twenty years of travel. This travel brought her into contact with mystic traditions and teachers all over the world. She claims they selected her to spread the teachings of theosophy.

Her travels and subsistence were financed by a family friend who sent her money. It is said that she was a pianist of some note and performed concerts for income. One can be sure that she did not have to work as most people do. She grew up in luxury and managed to live the majority of her life without the need to labor.

Later in life, she made acquaintance with Vsevolod Sergueyevich Solovyov. She described him to a friend as being a true theosophist. It is apparent that she esteemed him. Interestingly, though, Solovyov wrote of Blavatsky in several articles published both in Russia and England. In the preface to one article titled *A Modern Priestess of Isis*, Professor Sidgwick, an acquaintance of Solovyov wrote that readers:

> **...would not so much desire additional proof**
> **that [Blavatsky] was a charlatan—a question**

The Millennium Agenda

> already judged and decided—but rather
> some explanation of the remarkable success
> of her imposture; and...her supple craft and
> reckless audacity.[112]

A charlatan is a person who pretends to have expert knowledge. Sidgwick, it would appear, esteemed his colleague, Solovyov, but had little regard for Blavatsky. And it is likely that even Solovyov did not hold Blavatsky in the same esteem as she did him.

Among her writings, Blavatsky speaks of the Bible in a point that she makes about Jesus being a mystic. She points out the passage in Mark Chapter 4:

> [Jesus] told them, "The secret of the king-
> dom of God has been given to you. But to
> those on the outside everything is said in
> parables...(Mark 4:11 NIV)

She leaves out the second part of the sentence:

> "...so that, 'they may be ever seeing but
> never perceiving, and ever hearing but
> never understanding; otherwise they might
> turn and be forgiven!' "(Mark 4:12 NIV).

This is very likely Jesus' remembrance of the prophecy to Isaiah. In this prophecy, Isaiah is told of the destruction of the Jews because of their hard hearts.

> [God] said, "Go and tell this people: 'Be ever
> hearing, but never understanding; be ever
> seeing, but never perceiving' "(Isaiah 6:9
> NIV).

 Likewise, the Jews of Jesus' day heard but did not understand, they saw but did not believe. Verse 12 of Mark 4 is not a declaration, but rather an observation. Paul told the Corinthians that God's wisdom would confound the wise:

> For it is written: "I will destroy the wisdom
> of the wise; the intelligence of the intelligent
> I will frustrate."
>
> Where is the wise man? Where is the

scholar? Where is the philosopher of this age? Has not God made foolish the wisdom of the world? (I Corinthians 1:19-20 NIV)

So it is with Blavatsky. Jesus' reference to "mysteries" was His explanation for the use of parables. His claim was that the truths of the gospel would be too complex for people to grasp on first encounter. By giving them a parable, they could reflect on the parable and come to understand the gospel in its fullest.

Blavatsky seems to take delight in pointing out that the wise men, or magi, who saw the star that led them to the infant Jesus, were magicians. The Latin word for "magician" is *magi*. While they may have been magicians, their inclusion in the Bible is not to be construed as an endorsement of magic.

She defines magic as white and black. White magic, she claims, is the magic used to benefit humankind while black magic is that used for one's own gratification. The Bible makes no distinction.

Sylvia Cranston, in a biography about Blavatsky, says that in about 1873 Blavatsky began establishing her work. Cranston states:

> **At first [Blavatsky] attempted to interest the Spiritualists in the philosophy behind phenomena but they resented her refusal to accept their standard explanations.**[113]

Blavatsky was such a loose cannon that even the occultists wouldn't accept her ideas. Later in the same year, she established the Theosophical Society along with H. S. Olcott and W. Q. Judge. The Theosophical Society's stated objective is " humanitarian and educational."[114] However, it is clear from reading any of her material that it is clearly religious.

> **In 1878 she and H. S. Olcott left for India. There they worked to re-establish Oriental philosophical and religious ideas.**[115]

William Quan Judge was an Irish emigrant. He specialized in corporate law in New York. Henry Steel Olcott was born in New Jersey and was a journalist. He also practiced law and later returned to the journalism field reporting on spiritualistic phenomena.

In her first book, *Isis Unveiled*, Blavatsky pointed out the similarities between the world's mythologies and the perennial philosophy underlying the world's religious traditions. Volume one focused on science and its limitations and truths. Volume two examines creeds, religions, and mythologies past and present.[116] While it may be true that all religions share common tenets, they cannot (and should not) be categorically considered to be of singular origin. Isis, by the way, is an Egyptian goddess of fertility.

In 1885, Blavatsky began work on *The Secret Doctrine* while living in Europe. In 1887, she moved to London and began a magazine entitled *Lucifer*. Blavatsky describes the origin of the word "theosophy":

> **The word theosophy has been used in the Occident for about 2,000 years to indicate knowledge of divine things or knowledge derived from insight and experience as well as intellectual study.**[117]

Incidentally, Hitler kept *The Secret Doctrine* at his bedside and practiced its philosophies faithfully throughout his reign as the leader of the Nazi-German war machine. Many of the philosophies that he proposed (the Aryan race, for instance) were drawn directly from the pages of Blavatsky's book.

Theosophy

The word "theosophy" comes from the Greek theos (god, divinity) and sophia (wisdom), and translates as divine wisdom. This wisdom is intended to mean the inner divine wisdom that every person contains and can draw from. Do not confuse this term to imply that the individual receives this divine wisdom from God, the Holy Spirit, or from prayer. The word "theosophy" specifically proposes the idea of divine wisdom generated from within man.

Theosophical concepts are not dogmas; only

> **the ideas that have value need be accepted.
> Theosophical books are considered neither
> as revelation nor final authority, but as
> guides in the individual's search. However,
> there are some basic concepts that theoso-
> phy brings to light.**[118]

As you can see from this quote of Blavatsky, there are no moral absolutes. Note also, that one only needs to believe, or exercise those "ideas that have value." This is the cafeteria-style doctrine that was discussed earlier in this book. In my mind, a concept is either true or false. Everyone should adhere to a doctrine because of its divine truth, or flee from it because of its evil intent.

This "divine wisdom" is that concerning all things in light of "divine consciousness." Again, a term which does not refer to an omniscient god, but rather to the "essential oneness of all beings."

The concept is similar to that of Buddhism, in which all things are part of this great conglomerate of life; each individual element, even the atoms, are as much alive as you or I. Stones, trees, and planets, and the universe itself comprise life. Life is not limited to those organisms which we typically think of as "alive." Theosophy thus considers everything alive. And since all is life, and all is one, then all must be divine.

> **Each is divine at its root and expresses itself
> through spiritual, intellectual, psychological,
> ethereal, and material ranges of conscious-
> ness and substance.**[119]

Since, then, all is life and all is divine, evolution fits into the picture with little effort. Evolution, theosophists claim, "reflects [an] emerging self-expression." In other words, inanimate objects can become animate objects because they are both "living." Lower living things can always become higher living things because of their Karma. And higher living things can become divine based on their Karma. And since all things are one, then all things are divine.

We, being divine, then are free, and in fact obligated, to choose for ourselves what is truth. Again, there is no moral absolute.

The Millennium Agenda

> As beings rooted in divinity, we each have
> the ability to discover reality for ourselves.
> To do this we must learn to judge what is
> true and false, real and illusory; not blindly
> follow the dictates of authority, however
> high.[120]

Theosophy forbids evangelism. This is an easy concept for theosophists to adopt since the philosophy is a come-as-you-are doctrine. There is no absolute basis for doctrinal truth. There are no absolute rights or wrongs.

> In following our own spiritual instincts and
> intuitions, we awaken our latent potentials.
> Trying to force others to adopt what we
> believe is the "proper" avenue of thought
> may be harmful. Everyone follows his or her
> own unique path of unfoldment (sic).[121]

The objective, then, is the improvement of all life. The way to improve all life is by improving our Karma. The way to improve our present Karma is through humanitarian service:

> The ideal is to put the welfare of humanity
> and all that lives ahead of one's own
> progress.[122]

And, in fact, a big part of the New Age movement deals with "good" things such as attempting to end world hunger, working toward world peace, and practicing environmental responsibility. This is most likely why the New Age has gained such public acceptance. These issues are not the problem with the New Age movement. Rather, the reason these issues are a concern to the New Age movement is the problem. The New Age teaches that we do these things to improve our Karma; to make us, and indeed all life, better—divine.

Karma, you may recall, is an Eastern religious concept based in Hindu, Buddhist, and other Eastern religions. Theosophy disputes the idea that Karma and reincarnation are exclusively Eastern, and even ascribes the idea of reincarnation to Judaism and Christianity.

> Although considered Oriental, reincarnation

was present in many traditions including Platonic philosophy, Judaism, and early Christianity.[123]

Keep in mind that although the authors of theosophy are quite ignorant of the spirit of Christian doctrine, they are well aware and well educated as to the text and words of the Bible. For instance, when they read passages that refer to resurrection, they immediately relate this to Eastern concepts of reincarnation.

Neither Judaism nor Christianity have ever advocated an iterative process of birth and rebirth, or reincarnation. The idea of resurrection is that we shall live again only by the grace of God who has renewed our physical bodies as pure. The blood of Jesus bought that renewal. That renewal is required only once to be sufficient for all history.

Blavatsky echoed John 7:16 saying that the work she was doing was not her own, but that of the one who sent her. The passage in John reflects Jesus' answer to the scholars who wanted to know how He came by such knowledge.

Jesus answered, "My teaching is not my own. It comes from him who sent me" (John 7:16 NIV).

Blavatsky does not explain the context of the quote, and leaves out the following statement, which is germane to the context of Jesus' answer.

If anyone chooses to do God's will, he will find out whether my teaching comes from God or whether I speak on my own. He who speaks on his own does so to gain honor for himself, but he who works for the honor of the one who sent him is a man of truth; there is nothing false about him (John 7:17-18 NIV).

Blavatsky set about with the express objective of establishing the Theosophical Society—an organization that she headed. As seen from earlier quotes, she is called a charlatan, and her bravado was well established.

The Millennium Agenda

Judging by her work, I would say she was sent by Satan. It was not uncommon for occult writers of the late 19th and early 20th century to toss in tidbits of biblical scripture in an attempt to give their message some authenticity. It is also somewhat annoying when they make references totally out of context or use a quote that is so benign as to not convey any meaning on its own.

Speaking of salvation, theosophy teaches that man is his own salvation:

> **We are responsible for our own lives. No one else—divine or human—can take away or neutralize the results of any of our actions.**[124]

I cannot think of a more insulting, sacreligious statement that can be made by any human.

Paul wrote to the Colossians about false teachers:

> **See to it that no one takes you captive through hollow and deceptive philosophy, which depends on human tradition and the basic principles of this world rather than on Christ (Colossians 2:8 NIV).**

The early Christian church was battling gnosticism. This is a religious belief that neutralized Jesus as deity and made various other claims that did not conform to the teachings of Christ. Paul addressed this by identifying the nature of the religion. It is based on traditions (or pagan rituals), on human reason, and on science (physical and natural science of the day).

This same situation is present today—particularly that of human reason. Since man cannot understand the ways of God, he therefore endeavors to neutralize God's miraculous power by ascribing His work to presumptions of science and at the same time intermingling pagan tradition into Christian worship.

Presumptions of science would be things like evolution, which cannot be proven. However, it allows the human mind an escape from accepting the creative power of God.

> As I urged you when I went into Macedonia,
> stay there in Ephesus so that you may com-
> mand certain men not to teach false doc-
> trines any longer nor to devote themselves
> to myths and endless genealogies. These
> promote controversies rather than God's
> work—which is by faith (I Timothy 1:3-4
> NIV).

The teachings of Blavatsky and others are clearly based on ancient pagan rituals and mythology. The fact that Blavatsky titled one of her books *Isis Revealed* is a testament to her reverence of Egyptian mythology.

> The Spirit clearly says that in later times
> some will abandon the faith and follow
> deceiving spirits and things taught by
> demons.
>
> Such teachings come through hypocritical
> liars, whose consciences have been seared as
> with a hot iron (I Timothy 4:1-2 NIV).

The main reason that men try so hard to invent scientific explanations for God's actions is because at the root of their being, they hate the truth. Some scientists and philosophers claim to be seekers of truth; however, they make great efforts to thwart the truth of God's handiwork and the gospel of Jesus.

> The coming of the lawless one will be in
> accordance with the work of Satan displayed
> in all kinds of counterfeit miracles, signs and
> wonders, and in every sort of evil that de-
> ceives those who are perishing. They perish
> because they refused to love the truth and so
> be saved.
>
> For this reason God sends them a powerful
> delusion so that they will believe the lie and
> so that all will be condemned who have not
> believed the truth but have delighted in
> wickedness (II Thessalonians 2:9-12 NIV).

The Millennium Agenda

This tells us that in the end times many will deny—in fact, hate—the truth of the gospel. We are also told that those who hate the gospel will then be given a "delusion," a *false truth* that will be their end. False teachers abound today as they did in the days of the early Christian church.

Alice A. Bailey

Alice Bateman met a man in 1895 who told her that her life would require a change in order to carry out the work for which she was chosen. She was fifteen. At the age of thirty, she was introduced to theosophy at Pacific Grove, California. Through her study of Blavatsky's *The Secret Doctrine*, Alice concluded that the man she met when she was fifteen was not Jesus, as she had presumed. The mysterious man was Koot Hoomi, whom she refers to as Master KH. The work and writings that she authored, she claims, were the result of telepathic contact with Master DK (Djwhal Khul).

She later met and married Foster Bailey. She started the Lucifer Trust in 1922. The purpose of the Lucifer Trust was to establish a "New World Order." The name Lucifer was specifically chosen to represent Satan, who led the revolt in heaven before his fall. She later changed the name to Lucis Trust due to the obvious controversy surrounding the name Lucifer.

In 1932, Bailey started the World Goodwill, an organization whose goal was to create a one-world religion and government. This organization works closely with the United Nations.

Alice Bailey explains:

> **When speaking of the Christ we are refer-ring to His official name as Head of the Hierarchy. The Christ works for all men and does not belong to any one religion. He belongs to all religions as much as He does to Christianity. To be affiliated to the Christ does not require any person to join the Christian church.**[125]

While it is true that Jesus' appeal was to all men, both Jew and

Gentile, this quote above is the craftiest attack that I have ever heard. The statement is technically true. A person does not necessarily need to be a member of a "Christian" church to be affiliated with the Christ. But, what does one need to do to be affiliated to the Christ? Jesus Himself said:

> **Whoever acknowledges me before men, I will also acknowledge him before my Father in heaven (Matthew 10:32 NIV).**

Bailey goes on to explain that Jesus and "The Christ" are separate entities—that Jesus, the "great Brother" of the Christ is "the inspirer or director of the Christian Church."[126] Satan, in his usual style, has flooded the second coming of Jesus with a number of counterfeits. Some expect Maitreya, others Bodhisattva, and yet others expect Imam Mahdi. All of these are counterfeit christs which are expected by various religions.

Bailey then explains just how the Christ will appear. High-speed transit, mass communication and such will of course facilitate this:

> **He will not come as an omnipotent God, as triumphant warrior or conquering hero.**
> **Nor will He come as the Messiah of the Jews to save the Holy Land because He belongs to the whole world.**[127]

This quote is consistent with a great deal of Bailey's writings—a direct contradiction of biblical teaching. The book of Revelation explains the coming of Jesus as a miraculous, glorious event; an event that will be known to all humans because it will display His divinity, His authority, and His majesty.

However, the most annoying thing that I found about Bailey's teachings is how she consistently intermingles biblical messages with her teachings and misquotes scripture to convey a satanic message. Bailey's message is a prime example of the seed which "fell on rocky places."

> **A farmer went out to sow his seed. As he was scattering the seed, some fell along the path, and the birds came and ate it up. Some**

> fell on rocky places, where it did not have
> much soil. It sprang up quickly, because the
> soil was shallow. But when the sun came up,
> the plants were scorched, and they withered
> because they had no root. Other seed fell
> among thorns, which grew up and choked
> the plants. Still other seed fell on good soil,
> where it produced a crop—a hundred, sixty
> or thirty times what was sown (Matthew
> 13:3-8 NIV).

There are and will be many Christians who will come across
Bailey's material. Upon reading it, they may not examine it
against the scripture. They will see the scriptural references, be
confused by the biblical jargon, and thus believe it and be snared
by Satan. Her scriptural references are usually in the form of a
short phrase that does not even convey any meaning:

> He is expected as "coming in the clouds of
> the sky" but this may mean His coming by
> Aeroplane (sic) from the place where He has
> been for generations. He will play His part
> before the eyes of the entire world through
> radio and television.[128]

The quote "coming in the clouds of the sky" is from Matthew
26:64. She does not state which translation. The entire verse
reads:

> "Yes, it is as you say," Jesus replied. "But I
> say to all of you: In the future you will see
> the Son of Man sitting at the right hand of
> the Mighty One and coming on the clouds of
> heaven" (Matthew 26:64 NIV).

In this particular case, she uses the excerpt in a consistent
context, but to diminish the omnipotence of Jesus. In other cases,
the excerpt has little or nothing to do with the context of the
scripture from which it was taken.

And what adds to the problem is that this doctrine requires no
commitment by the reader. The gospel of Jesus calls us to
obedience. It calls us to worship and witness. The doctrine of

Bailey tells the reader that he or she is "saved" simply by being a good person—by loving everyone.

Lucifer

I wanted to address the name Lucifer since both Alice Bailey and Helena Blavatsky used the name for their publications.

The only reference to the word "Lucifer" in the Bible is in the book of Isaiah:

> **How art thou fallen from heaven, O Lucifer, son of the morning! how art thou cut down to the ground, which didst weaken the nations! (Isaiah 14:12 KJV)**

And "Lucifer" only appears in the *King James Version*. The translators of the *King James Version* of the Bible translated the Hebrew phrase into the Latin word "Lucifer." Most contemporary translations translate the Hebrew more literally. The *New International Version* reads:

> **How you have fallen from heaven, O morning star, son of the dawn! You have been cast down to the earth, you who once laid low the nations! (Isaiah 14:12 NIV)**

Blavatsky, Bailey, and others are correct in their translation of "Lucifer" to mean "light bringer." The literal translation, however, is "day star."

Lucifer, that is, Satan, was created as a being of beauty.

> **Son of man, take up a lament concerning the king of Tyre and say to him: "This is what the Sovereign LORD says: 'You were the model of perfection, full of wisdom and perfect in beauty.**
>
> **" 'You were in Eden, the garden of God; every precious stone adorned you: ruby, topaz and emerald, chrysolite, onyx and jasper, sapphire, turquoise and beryl. Your settings and mountings were made of gold;**

> on the day you were created they were
> prepared. You were anointed as a guardian
> cherub, for so I ordained you. You were on
> the holy mount of God; you walked among
> the fiery stones. You were blameless in your
> ways from the day you were created till
> wickedness was found in you' " (Ezekiel
> 28:12-15 NIV).

Although this passage addresses the "king of Tyre," it is commonly agreed that the passage refers to Satan. Tyre was a notoriously wicked city.

> You said in your heart, "I will ascend to
> heaven; I will raise my throne above the
> stars of God; I will sit enthroned on the
> mount of assembly, on the utmost heights of
> the sacred mountain. I will ascend above
> the tops of the clouds; I will make myself like
> the Most High" (Isaiah 14:13-14 NIV).

Chapter 12: Would the "Real" Christ Please Stand Up

One of the most common diversions from Jesus is the introduction of different Christ figures. Jesus knew this would happen and warned us:

> **For false Christs and false prophets will appear and perform great signs and miracles to deceive even the elect—if that were possible (Matthew 24:24 NIV).**

Further, He said:

> **I am the way and the truth and the life. No one comes to the Father except through me (John 14:6 NIV).**

Send in the Clowns

Many people are proposing an alternative Christ. It's not that they are denying that Jesus lived, or even that He is the Christ, but they are adding more to the story. Consider this passage from *Of Life and Other Worlds* by Aart Jurriaanse:

> **Most people are well acquainted with the history of Jesus Christ Who was born nearly two thousand years ago in Palestine. There are, however, some aspects of His life that are not so commonly known and which date back to long before the period of His biblical life on Earth. It should be realised (sic) that the Entity who made His appearance on Earth two millennia ago, must already have had a long preceding course of development to enable Him to attain such an advanced state of enlightenment.**[129]

I hope you caught the buzzword "enlightenment." This passage is telling us that Jesus is a reincarnated being. As Christians, we believe Jesus to simply be God *incarnate*. This passage describes Him in terms of the cycle of reincarnation; specifically the Hindu religious cycle in which one attains greater and greater enlightenment from life to life.

The Millennium Agenda

Apollonius of Tyana

In an Internet site I came across, Bette Stockbauer described Jesus as a "fourth-degree initiate" and claims that "in His next incarnation, as Apollonius of Tyana (16 AD to c. 97 AD), He became a Master (fifth-degree initiate). He died in India."[130]

> **The Master Jesus,...reached His state of perfection in the course of His next life as Apollonius of Tyana. Many of those who followed Him during his life as Jesus were still alive during his subsequent incarnation—and many of them became convinced that Jesus had reappeared in their midst. (Peter Liefhebber)**[131]

This says that Jesus was *not* perfect in His life. In fact, He only reached perfection *after* He was reincarnated another time. This is clearly contrary to the Bible which tells us that Jesus was sinless.

> **For we do not have a high priest who is unable to sympathize with our weaknesses, but we have one who has been tempted in every way, just as we are—yet was without sin (Hebrews 4:15 NIV).**

> **God made him who had no sin to be sin for us, so that in him we might become the righteousness of God (II Corinthians 5:21 NIV).**

It is important to believe this point. For if Jesus was imperfect, that is, if He had sin, then **He could not die for our sin.** It is also important to believe in the resurrection of Jesus, as cited earlier:

> **And if Christ has not been raised, our preaching is useless and so is your faith (I Corinthians 15:14 NIV).**

> **And if Christ has not been raised, your faith is futile; you are still in your sins (I Corinthians 15:17 NIV).**

Would the "Real" Christ Please Stand Up?

The Internet site continues by telling of the life of Apollonius. This individual was born of affluent parents and had the luxury of training and was able to study Pythagoras. The majority of information we have about Apollonius comes from the writings of Damis, who was a disciple and companion of Apollonius.

We know little of the philosophical teachings of Pythagoras. He is, however, most famous for his mathematical theorems; most notably, the Pythagorean theorem which calculates the hypotenuse of a right triangle. His followers continued his mathematical exploration even to an extreme. "They taught that the essence of all things was number and that all relationships—even abstract concepts like justice—could be expressed numerically."[133]

> **Pythagoras** c.582–c.507 B.C., pre-Socratic Greek philosopher. We know little of his life and nothing of his writings; all of our knowledge comes from his followers, the Pythagoreans, a mystical brotherhood he founded at Crotona. Members of the order regarded Pythagoras as a demigod and attributed all their doctrines to him.[132]

However, if we consider the information about Apollonius to be true, then should we not consider Pythagoras as greater than Apollonius, since Apollonius learned from Pythagoras? Pythagoras' followers were involved in some kind of cult which considered him a demigod (the term literally refers to the offspring of a human and a god, but can refer to someone who exhibits godlike powers who is not a god). Cults, by definition, are secretive and covert. Jesus, on the other hand, did nothing in secret.

> **"I have spoken openly to the world," Jesus replied. "I always taught in synagogues or at the temple, where all the Jews come together. I said nothing in secret" (John 18:20 NIV).**

Other than the Internet information, I am unable to find any

The Millennium Agenda

historical evidence of Apollonius of Tyana. It appears that the *only* information available was written within the last century. The accounts of Jesus, on the other hand, are documented not only in the scriptures, but also in eyewitness manuscripts that have been discovered. Josephus, the secular historian who lived in Jesus' time, also makes mention of Jesus:

> **Now, there was about this time Jesus, a wise man, if it be lawful to call him a man, for he was a doer of wonderful works—a teacher of such men as receive the truth with pleasure. He drew over to him both many of the Jews, and many of the Gentiles. He was [the] Christ; and when Pilate, at the suggestion of the principal men amongst us, had condemned him to the cross, those that loved him at the first did not forsake him, for he appeared to them alive again the third day, as the divine prophets had foretold these and ten thousand other wonderful things concerning him; and the tribe of Christians, so named from him, are not extinct at this day (Josephus 18.3.3).** [134]

But, let's get back to the New Age. Aart Jurriaanse states:

> **To describe the Christ merely as a Son of God is rather meaningless and inadequate, because we are really all children of God (even though many may not seem to act accordingly). The outstanding difference between the Christ and the other members of the human family was that by His rapid rate of progress He outstripped all His contemporaries on the Path of Life....**
>
> **He was the first human being to reach perfection and to pass on to the spiritual kingdom.** [135]

Now, this passage just told you that Jesus was no more, no less, than you or I, and that He simply utilized His time and energies more efficiently that we. And more:

Would the "Real" Christ Please Stand Up?

> The personality is perishable and disinte-
> grates after "death," whilst the soul is im-
> mortal and continues its spiritual existence,
> having learnt further lessons in its earthly
> shell. The crucifixion of Jesus the Christ
> must be regarded in a similar light. The
> physical body of Jesus was sacrificed but the
> real Christ, the spiritual aspect, could of
> course never be physically nailed to the
> cross.[136]

The author now tells you that the cross wasn't that big of a deal—
simply extinguishing the flesh has no effect on the soul.

There seems to be no end to this drivel. I scan the Internet and
am flooded with information. After a few seconds of reading the
material, I become aware of its occult and satanic origin.

Setting the Stage

By now, you may be wondering how this all ties together. Well,
quite simply, all this confusion is setting the stage for the
appearance of the antichrist. I guess what is most frightening to
me is that it points to specific people who are alive today.

In particular, I found some information on the Internet from an
organization called Share International which advocates a person
named Maitreya as the Christ.

All of the peripheral teachings about Maitreya suggest that he
will require other teachers and leaders to identify him to the
public as the Christ. Other writings clearly show that he is *not*
God. He will demonstrate only minimal miracles, if any.
Otherwise, he will require modern technology to accomplish what
the Bible claims about the second coming of Christ. Specifically,
his followers claim that mass media will fulfill the scripture:

> Look, he is coming with the clouds, and
> every eye will see him, even those who
> pierced him; and all the peoples of the earth
> will mourn because of him. So shall it be!
> Amen (Revelation 1:7 NIV).

The Millennium Agenda

They also claim that "coming with the clouds" is a reference to commercial aviation. The antichrist will require a plane to get about.

Many people (and possibly Maitreya himself) believe that Maitreya is Jesus reincarnated. At this point, I can only remind you of the words of Jesus and the gospel as conveyed by His apostles:

> Jesus answered, "I am the way and the truth and the life. No one comes to the Father except through me. If you really knew me, you would know my Father as well. From now on, you do know him and have seen him" (John 14:6-7 NIV).

> Don't you believe that I am in the Father, and that the Father is in me? The words I say to you are not just my own. Rather, it is the Father, living in me, who is doing his work (John 14:10 NIV).

> I am the gate; whoever enters through me will be saved. He will come in and go out, and find pasture. The thief comes only to steal and kill and destroy; I have come that they may have life, and have it to the full (John 10:9-10 NIV).

> For God did not send his Son into the world to condemn the world, but to save the world through him. Whoever believes in him is not condemned, but whoever does not believe stands condemned already because he has not believed in the name of *God's one and only Son* (emphasis added) (John 3:17-18 NIV).

> Then Jesus declared, "I am the bread of life. He who comes to me will never go hungry, and he who believes in me will never be

> thirsty. But as I told you, you have seen me
> and still you do not believe. All that the
> Father gives me will come to me, and who-
> ever comes to me I will never drive away.
> For I have come down from heaven not to do
> my will but to do the will of him who sent
> me. And this is the will of him who sent me,
> that I shall lose none of all that he has given
> me, but raise them up at the last day. For
> my Father's will is that everyone who looks
> to the Son and believes in him shall have
> eternal life, and I will raise him up at the
> last day" **(John 6:35-40 NIV)**.

Jesus made claims and declarations such as "Take heart, son; your sins are forgiven" (Matthew 9:2 NIV), that only God is entitled to make. This is why the Jewish leaders wanted to have him executed. Their charge was blasphemy, which is defined as "the act of claiming for oneself the attributes and rights of God."[137]

For Jesus to "forgive" sin, the sin must have been committed against *Him*. No man can forgive a debt which is owed to someone else, and therefore, if Jesus was forgiving sin, then He was acting as God.

The Islamic religion does not recognize Jesus as God for two reasons. First, they find the pluralism unconscionable, believing it is impossible for someone to be both God and man. Secondly, they believe that Jesus never claimed, in His own words, to be God (i.e., "I am God"). This second statement is technically true. The following passages show how Jesus did, in fact, assert His divinity:

While speaking with the apostles, Jesus addresses Peter:

> **"But what about you?"** he asked. **"Who do
> you say I am?"** Simon Peter answered, **"You
> are the Christ, the Son of the living God."**
>
> Jesus replied, **"Blessed are you, Simon son of
> Jonah, for this was not revealed to you by**

man, but by my Father in heaven" (Matthew
16:15-17 NIV).

When Jesus was speaking with the Samaritan woman at the well:

The woman said, "I know that Messiah"
(called Christ) "is coming. When he comes,
he will explain everything to us."

Then Jesus declared, "I who speak to you am
he" (John 4:25-26 NIV).

Possibly the strongest statement by Jesus is this made to the
apostle John in the Revelation:

"I am the Alpha and the Omega," says the
Lord God, "who is, and who was, and who is
to come, the Almighty" (Revelation 1:8 NIV).

Remember on one occasion that Jesus was actually accused of
being satanic. He had been casting out demons. To this
accusation, He answered:

Every kingdom divided against itself will be
ruined, and every city or household divided
against itself will not stand. If Satan drives
out Satan, he is divided against himself. How
then can his kingdom stand?

And if I drive out demons by Beelzebub, by
whom do your people drive them out? So
then, they will be your judges. But if I drive
out demons by the Spirit of God, then the
kingdom of God has come upon you (Matthew 12:25-28 NIV).

In this particular passage, the Jewish leaders actually attempt to
stone Jesus for His claims to be the Christ.

The Jews gathered around him, saying,
"How long will you keep us in suspense? If
you are the Christ, tell us plainly."

Jesus answered, "I did tell you, but you do
not believe. The miracles I do in my Father's

> name speak for me, but you do not believe
> because you are not my sheep. My sheep
> listen to my voice; I know them, and they
> follow me. I give them eternal life, and they
> shall never perish; no one can snatch them
> out of my hand.
>
> My Father, who has given them to me, is
> greater than all; no one can snatch them out
> of my Father's hand. *I and the Father are
> one.*"
>
> Again the Jews picked up stones to stone
> him, but Jesus said to them, "I have shown
> you many great miracles from the Father.
> For which of these do you stone me?"
>
> "We are not stoning you for any of these,"
> replied the Jews, "but for blasphemy, be-
> cause you, a mere man, claim to be God"
> (John 10:24-33 NIV, italics added).

So you see, while Jesus may never have actually uttered the words, "I am God," it is clear from the reactions of the Jews that He did not leave any doubt that He was presenting Himself as God. Public stoning was a most immediate and severe punishment for blasphemy. This may be why Jesus always demonstrated His divinity in parables. He did not want to be executed before all of the prophecies concerning Him had been fulfilled.

His final act of deity came on His resurrection. Many believe that His resurrection merely represents His power over death. It should be noted, however, that when Jesus died, He carried the sin debt of the entire world with Him. That debt had to be settled. Some scholars believe that Jesus physically went to hell to deliver our sin. Thus His resurrection shows us that He was able to leave our sins in hell and return to His rightful seat in heaven sinless and perfect.

When Jesus returns to earth no one will need to tell you. No one

The Millennium Agenda

will need to identify Him. No one will need to prepare His way.

> **For as lightning that comes from the east is visible even in the west, so will be the coming of the Son of Man (Matthew 24:27 NIV).**

The apostle John records in the Revelation:

> **I saw heaven standing open and there before me was a white horse, whose rider is called Faithful and True. With justice he judges and makes war. His eyes are like blazing fire, and on his head are many crowns. He has a name written on him that no one knows but he himself. He is dressed in a robe dipped in blood, and his name is the Word of God.**
>
> **The armies of heaven were following him, riding on white horses and dressed in fine linen, white and clean. Out of his mouth comes a sharp sword with which to strike down the nations. "He will rule them with an iron scepter." He treads the winepress of the fury of the wrath of God Almighty.**
>
> **On his robe and on his thigh he has this name written: KING OF KINGS AND LORD OF LORDS (Revelation 19:11-16 NIV).**

The appearance of the horseman comes after the tribulation in John's vision. The horseman is Jesus, poised ready to reclaim the earth. We know Jesus as loving, kind, forgiving. However, a day is approaching when justice is demanded. On that day, Jesus will act as executioner. He stands at the gate of heaven ready with His army to cut down the idolatrous, evil nations and rulers. He will measure out justice with exactitude. There will be no more mercy.

> **Then I saw the beast and the kings of the earth and their armies gathered together to make war against the rider on the horse and his army.**

Would the "Real" Christ Please Stand Up?

But the beast was captured, and with him the false prophet who had performed the miraculous signs on his behalf. With these signs he had deluded those who had received the mark of the beast and worshiped his image. The two of them were thrown alive into the fiery lake of burning sulfur.

The rest of them were killed with the sword that came out of the mouth of the rider on the horse, and all the birds gorged themselves on their flesh (Revelation 19:19-21 NIV).

Then I saw a new heaven and a new earth, for the first heaven and the first earth had passed away, and there was no longer any sea. I saw the Holy City, the new Jerusalem, coming down out of heaven from God, prepared as a bride beautifully dressed for her husband.

And I heard a loud voice from the throne saying, "Now the dwelling of God is with men, and he will live with them. They will be his people, and God himself will be with them and be their God. He will wipe every tear from their eyes. There will be no more death or mourning or crying or pain, for the old order of things has passed away" (Revelation 21:1-4 NIV).

Jesus is our holy Savior. He alone stands in the gap between God the Father and us. Jesus is to be praised above all creation.

The apostle Paul wrote to the Colossians:

My purpose is that [all believers] may be encouraged in heart and united in love, so that they may have the full riches of complete understanding, in order that they may know the mystery of God, namely, Christ, in

> whom are hidden all the treasures of wisdom
> and knowledge.
>
> I tell you this so that no one may deceive you
> by fine-sounding arguments (Colossians 2:2-4
> NIV).

Paul seemed to understand the nature of the false gospels. They rely upon reason and clever argument rather than on sound theological doctrine. He continues:

> See to it that no one takes you captive
> through hollow and deceptive philosophy,
> which depends on human tradition and the
> basic principles of this world rather than on
> Christ (Colossians 2:8 NIV).

Secret Organizations

Secret organizations in general should be avoided. Any organization that keeps its rites or procedures a secret can pose a potential threat to Christianity. Jesus never did anything in secret. In fact, when pressured by the church leaders, He responded:

> **"I have spoken openly to the world," Jesus replied. "I always taught in synagogues or at the temple, where all the Jews come to-gether. I said nothing in secret" (John 18:20 NIV).**

If organizations are truly benevolent, then their inner workings should not need to be kept secret.

Masonic lodges and other "brotherhood" societies are very secretive about initiation rites and ceremonies. Even the Boy Scouts of America organization has rites and ceremonies which are conducted in secret, and the participants are forbidden to discuss them with anyone except other initiates.

I find myself skeptical of any organization that keeps secrets from the general public. I had a friend who had reached the Eagle Scout level of the Boy Scouts. Even though he opposed the principle of secretive organizations, he was steadfast in not sharing the secret initiation of the Eagle Scout.

The symbols of the Freemasons (left) and Shriners (center). I am intrigued by the similarity of the Shriner emblem and the symbol for Islam (right).

The Millennium Agenda

The Masons and Shriners have "temples" where they perform their rites and ceremonies. Some of their temples are named after pagan deities, Egyptian cities and figures, as well as ancient Hebrew cities. For instance, the Isis Temple in Salina, Kansas, and the Osiris Temple in Wheeling, West Virginia. Isis is an Egyptian goddess of fertility who married her brother, Osiris.

> **The worship of Isis, together with that of her brother and husband, OSIRIS, and their son, HORUS, resisted the rise of Christianity and lasted until the 6th cent. A.D.**[138]

The Shriner emblem on the previous page depicts a Turkish sword, a crescent around a star, and a shield on the crescent. The crescent symbolizes secrecy surrounding something. Since the star is within the crescent, one might perceive the star to represent the object of the secrecy. A five-pointed star is sometimes associated with Satan.

The Shriners is a branch organization of the Masonic order.

The Scottish Rite is also a branch organization that is designed for advanced Masonic members. It states of itself:

> **Neither Scottish in origin nor a rite in the religious sense, the Scottish Rite has as its ultimate goal mankind's moral and spiritual development.**[139]

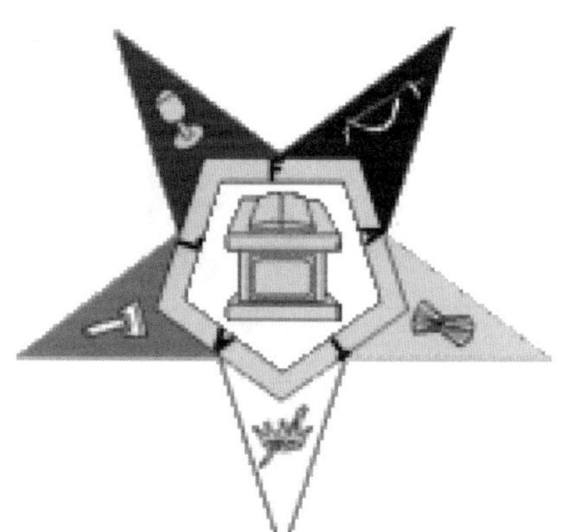

I find it interesting that it reputes to be secular, but seeks to develop the spirituality of its members.

Another organization related to the Masons is the Eastern Star (emblem at left):

The Order of the Eastern Star is a Masonically-related fraternity of women

> **and men dedicated to charity, truth and
> loving kindness. Although not a part of the
> Masonic fraternity, membership is based on
> a Masonic affiliation or relationship, a belief
> in God, and a desire to acquire additional
> knowledge and for self improvement.**[140]

This organization includes women whereas the Masonic lodge is exclusively male.

The emblem of the Eastern star, shown at left, is an inverted pentagram (upside-down five-pointed star), which is almost always associated with Satan. Each branch of the star contains some other symbolism that I cannot interpret.

The DeMolay order, also a branch organization of the Masonic lodge, is designed for youth. Its target membership age range is twelve to twenty-one and the youths must believe in a supreme being. It is not particular about which supreme being they believe in. An Internet site explained the symbolism of the DeMolay flag that consists of many different shapes among which is a crescent:

> **The crescent is a sign of secrecy and con-
> stantly reminds DeMolays of their duty
> never to reveal the secrets or betray the
> confidence of a friend.**[141]

Of its credo;

> **...the basic tenets and foundation of
> DeMolay. Those being: Love of God, Love of
> Home, and Love of Country.**[142]

Sounds wholesome enough; however, "god" is not defined. And since the organization is secretive, outsiders may have little knowledge of the true nature of the "god" that is revered by the DeMolays.

Another Internet site about the DeMolay organization contained information explaining the origin of the DeMolay order. It featured a page that was the story of Jacques DeMolay. The story gave a very romantic portrait not only of Jacques DeMolay, but

The Millennium Agenda

also of the Knights Templar, of which DeMolay was the Grand Master. The Knights Templar, which began as a militia of the Roman Catholic church, amassed great wealth. The secrecy around the location of the treasury is the basis for the bond of secrecy of the DeMolay organization. (Both the Masonic lodge and DeMolay order have their origin in the Knights Templar.) The story glorifies DeMolay's defiance of the French monarchy which attempted to force him to divulge the location of the Templars' treasury.

The Internet site does not mention that DeMolay and the Knights Templar had become corrupt. They were loyal only to the church (which had also become corrupt) and had no accountability to any government. This caused them to become arrogant and unruly. The Knights Templar oppressed the populace and DeMolay, as Grand Master, was held accountable for the Templars. According to public record, DeMolay was executed for defiling a cross, and doing so in public.

> **In 1314, Jacques de Molay was tried and convicted of blasphemy and treason. Among the accusations against him: That he and his Templars worshipped Baphomet, the satanic androgynous goat-god of Gnosticism.**
>
> **De Molay was also found guilty of homo-sexual perversions and of the blasphemous act of urinating on a crucifix of Christ.**[143]

Some Templars have defended this action claiming that this was their indignation and anger towards the role that the cross played in the death of Christ rather than their attitude toward Christ Himself. A crucifix, however, is a cross that bears the form of a man, representing Christ. Since the crucifix bears an image that represents Christ, DeMolay's actions would have been against the person of Christ, and not the cross alone.

Secrecy almost always surrounds satanic and occult rituals. Jesus proclaimed openness, for the truth will stand on its own. In fact, Jesus advocated publicly proclaiming the truth.

> **You are the light of the world. A city on a hill**

> **cannot be hidden. Neither do people light a
> lamp and put it under a bowl. Instead they
> put it on its stand, and it gives light to every-
> one in the house.**
>
> **In the same way, let your light shine before
> men, that they may see your good deeds and
> praise your Father in heaven (Matthew 5:14-
> 16 NIV).**

Anything that must be done secretly, or its rituals and ceremonies
kept secret, is missing the point about God's desire for His truth
to reach all men. The Hebrew nation was chosen by God to be the
ambassadors of His truth to the world. But rather than share the
truth of His redemption, they kept it to themselves—like putting
a lamp under a bowl.

Ironically, most of these organizations present themselves as
Christian in nature. They have crosses and crowns and other
Christian-looking symbols. However, their secretive nature is
inconsistent with the gospel. One organization claimed that it
was necessary for their members to be Christian because non-
Christians would not understand the ritual. This, no doubt, is the
public reason for the secrecy of all these organizations. The gothic
subculture today displays crosses as prominent symbols, but the
subculture is anything but holy.

I have found in my years at church, and in my personal witness,
that it is my Christian "peculiarity" that gives rise to my sharing
Christ. If Christians always hid their Christianity, then there
would be no evangelism. Further, Jesus came to earth to rid the
people of the heavy yoke of religious ritual. In fact, the Jewish
religious structure had become so complex that the common
person was simply unable to keep up with it. Jesus specifically
came to eliminate the complexity of the Jewish religion. Recall
the veil between the Holy of Holies and the Temple that was torn
in two when Jesus died. This veil was erected to protect man
from the holiness of God. Only the priest, after thorough ritual,
could enter. Even then, he had a bell attached to his garments
and a rope attached to his feet. If he was unclean, he would die in
the presence of God and the bell would stop ringing. The others

The Millennium Agenda

would pull him out by the rope.

Jesus also opposed secrecy of religion. When Jesus came to Earth, He specifically sent messengers not only to the Jews, but also to the Gentiles, so that all men could come to know Him.

The Priori de Sion

I had a manager who once said that one could make a graph of accounting information indicate anything, positive or negative, while depicting the exact same data. So it seems is the case with the Priori de Sion. This organization has managed to interpret history and the Bible to suit its own purpose. The Priori de Sion is the subject of a recent book entitled *Holy Blood, Holy Grail* by Michael Baigent.[144] The title hearkens to the romances of King Arthur and the Knights of the Roundtable. In actuality, the story put forth by Baigent is not far from fairy tale. The author claims to have come across a short novel while on a trip in Europe. He claims that the story begged for further investigation, and while it was presented as fiction, the story (according to Baigent) was true. He thus began to search for the heart of the "true" story.

With true journalistic style, he explores the story and proclaims that something was intentionally being held back or covered up. He and a few assistants then spent a great deal of effort and time examining what was being held secret from them. The root of the story was the Priori de Sion (the Priori of Sion). The story surrounding this group is so fantastic that there is no subtle way to introduce it.

Descendants of Jesus

In short, the members of the Priori de Sion are members of a family—a family that claims the right to rule not only France, but Jerusalem as well. This right, they claim, is based upon their lineage from Jesus. They claim to be direct descendants of Jesus. According to the Priori de Sion, Jesus was born to an aristocratic family. This family (Jesus' family) was the rightful heir to the Judaic throne by lineage of King David. As a Jewish teacher (Rabbi), Jesus was obligated to marry and His wedding, they claim, is the one mentioned in John Chapter 2. In this account,

Mary, Jesus' mother, asks Him to produce more wine since the guests are running out of it. Jesus obliges and this becomes His first recorded miracle.

Further, they claim that Jesus' wife was none other than Mary Magdalene. They claim that the image of Mary Magdalene was intentionally maligned by the Christian church to obscure this fact. Jesus and Mary then produced offspring, again as was expected of a Rabbi. Upon Jesus' trial and crucifixion (which they argue probably never happened), Mary Magdalene and the progeny escaped to the south of France while Jesus and His brother James stayed in the Holy Land to continue His work.

The southern part of modern France was the area occupied by the Merovingian dynasty. This dynasty claimed to be descended from the tribe of Benjamin. Thus, this would have been a Judaic community that would have given sanctuary to Mary Magdalene. The progeny of Mary and Jesus then intermarried with the Merovingians and became the bloodline now claimed by the Priori de Sion.

The accounts of the Grail, Baigent argues, are really a misnomer. He claims that the *"Sangraal"* as it is called in the Latin text is not "SAN GRAAL" (Holy Grail), but should be "SANG RAAL" (Blood Royal: Royal Blood). This, then, explains the legend of how Mary Magdalene brought the *Sangraal* (Holy Blood) to southern France and established the bloodline there. Joseph of Arimathea* apparently went to Britain, which is the claim of how the *Sangraal* (Holy Grail or Holy Blood) came to England and King Arthur's court.

How does Baigent arrive at Mary Magdalene being the wife of Jesus? This is based on the fact that a number of geographic sites, including churches, are dedicated to "The Magdalen": Mary Magdalene. In fact, it would seem that the French regions are preoccupied with The Magdalen. Interestingly enough, Baigent

---

* Some believe that Joseph of Arimathea, who was identified as wealthy in the Bible, was related to Jesus; perhaps his father-in-law.

The Millennium Agenda

admits:

> We were seeking fragments...In order to find them, we realized, we would be obliged to read between the lines, fill in certain gaps, account for certain [interruptions] and ellipses.[145]

He further adds regarding the idea of celibacy:*

> And, if Jesus did not preach celibacy, there is no reason to suppose that he practiced it.[146]

Holy Grail

There are several myths about what the Holy Grail really was. The most popular belief is that it was the cup that Jesus used at the Last Supper. Others believe that it was the cup or bowl that Joseph of Arimathea used to collect the blood of Jesus from the cross. Other myths describe the Holy Grail as a magical stone or as the bloodline of Jesus' descendants.

Baigent proceeds to explain why Mary Magdalene was Jesus' wife. He even suggests that Jesus performed a pagan ritual in the account where seven devils are cast out of Mary. He claims that Mary was probably "the disciple whom Jesus loved" (John 13:23 NIV), since this disciple is never named, and it is specifically the one that Jesus *loved*.

He further asserts:

> Could God claim to know the totality of Human existence without confronting the two such essential aspects of humanity as sexuality and paternity?[147]

The absurdity of this comment is beyond my understanding. The

---

* Celibacy of religious leaders was introduced by the Roman Catholic church several centuries after Jesus' death.

very definition of "God" includes omniscience—the ability to know all. Baigent is no doubt anthropomorphizing (giving human attributes to) God in this situation. Further, the purpose of God on earth, in the form of Jesus, wasn't to gain an understanding of the human experience—it was to redeem sinful humans from their sin debt.

Baigent also suggests that Jesus did not die on the cross, and that Barabbas (the thief who was released by Pilate in Matthew Chapter 27) was possibly even Jesus' son. He claims that the cry to "give us Barabbas!" was really a cry to "give us the son of ABBA!" He states that the word we translate and understand as a name, "Barabbas," is really two words: Bar Abba, which he further claims translates to "Son of Abba."

However, in my research, the word "bar" in the Hebrew refers to any kind of grain. It might loosely be construed to mean "seed" or "offspring" but this is not the common interpretation. Further, the New Testament manuscripts are in Greek or Aramaic—not Hebrew. Thus I find Baigent's argument for this alternate translation unconvincing.

The Merovingians

Baigent scrupulously researches the available resources. One must admire the fervor in which he approaches the topic. He gathers all sorts of information regarding the history of Europe. Some of the documents which Baigent uses are documents that are by no means considered factual or historical. Specifically, he uses the epic tales of Wolfram von Eschenbach, Sir Thomas Malory, Chrétien de Troyes, and their contemporaries. The epics of Eschenbach became the basis for some of Wagner's operas. They include all manner of mystery and romance. However, Baigent makes many excuses for using these as factual; primarily, that there is no documentation to refute them. We could, on similar bases, claim the story of Humpty Dumpty to be factual, since there is no refuting evidence.

On the other hand, he sharply criticizes the absence or scarcity of records of the church during the Dark Ages. He claims that this

The Millennium Agenda

lack of documentation is evidence of an obvious cover-up that was perpetrated by the Roman Catholic church to suppress evidence that it knew to be factual and damaging to the existence of the church. In other words, he believes that the church intentionally destroyed evidence and documentation that would prove Christianity a hoax. And while it might be true that the church actively attempted to destroy some documents, Baigent fails to acknowledge that the church would have done so as a means to eliminate spurious or errant doctrine. It may equally be true that organizations such as the Priori de Sion and religious sects manufactured or destroyed documentation in such a way to promote their own purposes. In so doing, it would be advantageous to throw suspicion on another organization to divert attention from the authenticity of the document itself. In other words, if everyone thinks that the document is a singular piece of evidence that survived a cover-up, then the attention would be on the alleged conspirator rather than on examining the authenticity of the alleged evidence.

Further, Baigent allows a great deal of flexibility to the ancient storytellers that he does not afford the Gospels. For instance, he admits that there are all sorts of dating errors, naming errors, and geographical errors which he manages to reconcile by taking liberties with the fictional material upon which he draws. Then when he addresses the text of the Gospels, he refuses to acknowledge that the differences in the Gospels are due to the fact that the writers are emphasizing different aspects of Jesus' ministry. He further dismisses the fact that so few documents exist upon which he has based his research, and equally ignores the plentitude of corroborating documents regarding the New Testament.

He draws upon speculation of customs on which to base his conclusions. In particular, he claims that Jesus could not have been placed in a tomb because the Roman government forbade executed (by crucifixion) criminals to be buried. This may be true in some cases. However, archaeologists found a grave in 1968 that bore the body of a man that had been crucified. The legs of the body had been severed because the 7½-inch spike which had been driven into the feet had hit a knot in the wood and could not be extracted with the body on the cross. Thus, the legs were severed and the spike pried loose. The spike remained in the feet in the grave.[148] Baigent also implies that the crucifixion was a private event that was not attended by the public, and not even by the family. I believe this to be complete speculation. Jesus addressed His mother from the cross, and His brother James as well. He also addressed one of the thieves on the other crosses. His cross bore the sign "King of the Jews." There would be no reason to have a sign on the cross if the event was, indeed, private. Furthermore, author Gary K. Halbrook explains:

> **During times of war and rebellion, little attention was paid to the way in which crucifixions were done. In peacetime, however, persons authorized by the Roman courts to perform crucifixions followed definite rules. Specific locations were designated for crucifixions; In Jerusalem, it was Golgatha.[149]**

Nevertheless, this alleged bloodline of Jesus' descendants is identified as the Merovingian bloodline after one Merovée (see inset).

Let's take a look at the origins of the Priori de Sion. In 1099, the

---

Merovingians, dynasty of Frankish kings that flourished from the 5th cent. to 751. They traced their descent from the semilegendary Merovech, or Meroveus, chief of the Salian Franks. His grandson, CLOVIS I, founded the Frankish monarchy in 481. His descendants divided his domains into Austrasia, Neustria, AQUITAINE, BURGUNDY, Paris, and Orléans. These territories were often combined and sometimes reunited under a single Merovingian ruler. Dagobert I (c.612–c.639) was the last Merovingian to exercise personal power. His successors, the "idle kings," left governing to the mayors of the palace, the CAROLINGIANS. In 751 PEPIN THE SHORT deposed Childeric III, the last Merovingian king.[150]

The Millennium Agenda

Merovingians, or, more specifically, Godfroi de Boullion (of the Merovingian bloodline), led a crusade that captured Western Palestine including Jerusalem. This is known as the first of the Crusades. A Latin capital was established in Jerusalem and the Priori de Sion was "officially" chartered in 1118. In 1187, the Saracens (Muslims) recaptured the region sending the Merovingians and the Priori de Sion back to France. The Priori de Sion has existed in differing forms ever since.

Among all the claims of the Priori de Sion members is an interesting array of world leaders:

> **We could even trace the Merovingian blood-line up to the present day—to Alain Poher, to Henri de Montpézat (consort of the queen of Denmark), to Pierre Plantard de Saint-Clair, to Otto von Hapsburg, titular duke of Lorraine and *king of Jerusalem*[151] (emphasis mine).**

Alain Poher won both the *Resistance Medal* and the *Croix de Guerre* during World War II. He also served as Provisional President of France from April 28 to June 19, 1969, and from April 2 to May 27, 1974.

Since the Merovingians are supposedly descended from Jesus, they believe that they will thus fulfill the prophecies of the New Jerusalem.

> **I saw the Holy City, the new Jerusalem, coming down out of heaven from God, prepared as a bride beautifully dressed for her husband (Revelation 21:2 NIV).**

In this passage, John implies that Jesus will be the husband. The Priori de Sion, since they claim to be descended from Jesus, expect thus to fulfill that prophecy. They want to establish the capital city of Jerusalem as the capital of the world. This is exactly what the book of Revelation tells us.

Furthermore, Baigent is obviously unaware of the way in which the Holy Spirit guides the hands and hearts of men. We believe that the hands of men that were guided by the Holy Spirit prepared the New Testament. Equally, the Holy Spirit guides those who read the New Testament. Someone once asked Jesus why He spoke in parables. He answered that the parables served to deliver the message in a way that requires divine interpretation. The gospel message requires the receiver to believe and anticipate the message. Those who do not believe the scripture cannot make sense of it. This appears to be the case with Baigent, who can only make sense of the scriptures if he takes all divinity out of it. Thus, he falls prey to the scripture that says the wisdom of God is foolishness to men.

The Millennium Agenda

Chapter 14: Is it Christian or Not?

The Roman Catholic Church

Let me start by saying that it is not my intention to imply that people who observe the Catholic doctrine are not Christian. Nor is my intention to imply that the Catholic church is not Christian. Rather, my intention is to point out some of the misguided ideology that has pervaded the upper echelon of the Roman Catholic church throughout the ages.

The Roman Catholic church began as a sect of the first century Christian church. However, due to certain interpretations, they became more sectarian and manipulative.

The idea of the Roman Catholic church being the "Head" of the church comes from several beliefs.

Peter was called the "rock" upon which Christ would build the church:

> **And I tell you that you are Peter, and on this rock I will build my church, and the gates of Hades will not overcome it (Matthew 16:18 NIV).**

Banias is believed to be the site where Jesus asked the disciples who He was. The site is significant because it was originally dedicated to the god Pan. The cavern in the center of the photo is one of the three sources of the Jordan River. The water bubbles up from the ground within the cave in the center. Just to the right is a carved niche which would have been a shrine to some graven image.

The Roman Catholic church then declared that Peter was the first pope. Thus, they ascribe to all popes the following power:

> **I will give you the keys of the kingdom of heaven; whatever you bind on earth will be bound in heaven, and whatever you loose on earth will be loosed in heaven (Matthew 16:19 NIV).**

Further, they declare that Peter established "the church" in Rome. I can find no biblical evidence that Peter established any church in Rome. Paul, however, did go to Rome, but you will recall that he was under house arrest and would hardly have been able to start or maintain a church.

Now, let's look at some of the basic precepts above. The Roman Catholic church, it appears, is careful to take certain verses as literal and certain as allegorical as is convenient for their purpose.

By declaring that Peter was the "rock" they believe that Peter, the man, was the person on which the church would be built. Recall the conversation leading up to verse 18 of Matthew 16 above. Jesus had just asked the disciples, "Who do men say that I am?" Among all the answers, Peter answered correctly: "You are the Christ!" Jesus then changed Peter's name (from Simon) and declared that upon this knowledge of Jesus as the Christ, would the church doctrine rest. Note how this differs from the literal translation.

It is not my intent to diminish Peter's role in the early church. No doubt Jesus' comment was also meant to convey that upon Peter's conviction (that Jesus *was* Christ), Peter would establish a mighty work for Christ.

Verse 19 is a statement of interest. I believe that this promise is given to all Christians. Here, the statement is given directly to Peter, because of his perception of Jesus. This understanding of Jesus as the Christ allows all Christians to exercise awesome power. Note a paraphrase of verse 19:

> **Whatsoever you declare to be bound on**

> **earth will be bound from heaven, and what-
> soever you declare to be loosed on earth will
> be loosed from heaven.**

I believe this to be the more accurate translation. This tells us that we have power given to us from our Father.

The Roman Catholic church translates the verse more literally as:

> **Whatsoever you declare on earth is therefore
> made so also in heaven, and whatsoever you
> loose on earth is therefore also loosed in
> heaven.**

This particular translation, they claim, gives the pope the power to add to or take away from the scripture. It also allows the pope to make any declaration, and thus declared, becomes part of the natural and supernatural order—as it were, scripture. For instance, in 1960, the pope made a statement that in effect said that Jesus' death was not necessary for our salvation.

Now, based upon these tenets, they further believe that the pope is second in authority only to Jesus. That is, the pope is the sole representative of God on Earth. Most people have a superficial understanding of this concept; however, let me not under-emphasize this. The Roman Catholic church believes that the pope acts and speaks for God on Earth—that God does nothing on Earth but through the pope.

> **The Pope alone is deservedly called by the
> name "most holy," because he alone is vicar
> of Christ....Hence the pope is crowned with a
> triple crown, as king of heaven and earth
> and of the lower regions....Moreover the
> superiority and the power of the Roman
> Pontiff by no means pertain only to heavenly
> things, to earthly things and to things under
> the earth, but are even over angels, than
> whom he is greater.**[152]

They further believe that the "Kingdom of God" on earth will be ruled (governed) by the pope. This was the cause for many fierce battles in the early centuries of Christendom over who would be pope. Indeed, there were many popes during the early centuries of the Roman Catholic church. They killed contenders, battled other candidates, and allied themselves with various earthly kingdoms as was convenient to gain military support.

> **Nearly all the wars which the northern barbarians carried on in Italy, it may be here remarked, were occasioned by the [popes]; and the hordes with which the country was inundated, were generally called in by them.**[153]

At one time, there were three persons from three different factions claiming to be pope. Benedict IX became pope at the age of eleven. His father "purchased" the papacy for him. His vices were apparent enough that a plot was laid to assassinate him. Hearing this, he fled, fell in love with a cousin, and sold the papacy to his uncle. Later he changed his mind and returned assuming the papacy. His uncle did not relinquish and a third contender also claimed the title:

> **[Benedict IX] held the Lateran Palace; Silvester [II] occupied St. Peter's and the Vatican Palace and Victor III [Benedict's uncle] had to be content with Sta. Maria Maggiore.**[154]

And, anyone could change the pope at will:

> **To finish with the long history of this phase of the Papal degradation, the pious new Emperor of Germany, Henry III, came to Rome, cleared out the three of them, and set Pope Clement II, an austere and virtuous prelate, upon the defiled and despised throne of the rulers of Papal Christendom— the "Holy See."**[155]

Earthly kings would assist a particular candidate for pope in return for certain political favors and vice versa. Even into the 14th century, the challenges for the papal throne left a pool of blood about the papal court.

The Roman Catholic church asserted its authority and would do

The Millennium Agenda

battle with other churches to force them to comply with their doctrine. The other churches (either in the right or wrong) resisted and followed their own doctrine. During various periods, the Roman Catholic church would subjugate other churches.

> **The first pastors or bishops of Rome enjoyed a respect proportionate to the rank of the city in which they resided. For the first few centuries of the Christian Era, Rome was the largest, richest, and most powerful city in the world...."If Rome is the queen of cities, why should not her pastor be the King of bishops?" was the reasoning these Roman pastors put forth.**[156]

In about 1400, the Roman Catholic church moved with Louis VII of France to abolish the Knights Templar, which as we discussed in Chapter 13, began as a Roman Catholic militia, and was responsible for the Crusades. In return, King Louis X made the Roman Catholic church the official church of France, thus abolishing all other churches (on punishment of death).

This was the most powerful boost for the Roman Catholic church. Some years later, King Henry VIII made a deal with the pope to make the Roman Catholic church officially The Church of England. In return, the pope bestowed the title of "Keeper of the Faith" upon Henry VIII. Shortly after, Henry VIII decided to divorce his first wife. The pope forbade this action, to which King Henry responded by creating the Protestant church (which would allow divorce). By the way, he kept the title of "Keeper of the Faith" and it now belongs to Queen Elizabeth II.

Throughout the years, the Roman Catholic church has made various declarations, particularly about science, which have been since proven false by practical science. The problem is that while the Bible states physical laws and evidences in very simplistic and self-evident fashion, the Roman Catholic church found it necessary to "explain" these manifestations and in so doing explained them with incomplete knowledge. As modern science learned more about nature and physics, the Roman Catholic "explanations" became invalidated by scientific discovery.

This is why you will see so many books and speakers claiming that Christianity is an elaborate hoax created by the Roman Catholic church for its own purpose. The idea that Christianity is a hoax is exacerbated by the fact that the Roman Catholic church has had to backtrack on many of its dogma over the many years of its existence. Unfortunately, the Roman Catholic church has painted itself into a corner. This is a problem of the Roman Catholic church and should not be ascribed to the entire Christian church.

Since the Roman Catholic church built this elaborate hoax, it finds itself in a precarious position now, vehemently defending its position, or compromising. And more often than not, it compromises. This last year, an interfaith conference was held in Dallas. The Cardinal Arinse (presumed to be the next pope) stated in humorous language that Jesus is not the only way to heaven, and that when Jesus declared Himself as the only way, He was referring that He was the only way for *Christians* (implying that means to salvation other than Jesus were just as valid).

The Roman Catholic church has conveniently removed the second commandment regarding idols.[157] Thus they venerate Mary and all other variety of saints and sites. They have split the tenth commandment (regarding coveting) into two to keep with the number ten. While Catholics will vehemently deny that they worship Mary or any saint, you will note that almost all of their prayers are addressed to Mary ("Hail Mary, full of grace...") or some other saint. Millions of people flock to see shrines of supposed Mary sightings (Our Lady of Guadalupe in Mexico,

Venerated sites include the church of the Annunciation in the modern city of Nazareth which was built by the Catholic church to mark the presumed location where Mary received the news of her soon-to-be baby, Jesus.

The Millennium Agenda

etc.).

These and many other sites in Israel have been venerated to the extent that their individual glory nearly eclipses the life and ministry of Jesus.

In his commentary on the book of Daniel, Uriah Smith explains a dream that King Nebuchadnezzar had. Daniel later had a similar dream with a similar interpretation. In Nebuchadnezzar's dream, there appeared four kingdoms. Nebechadnezzar saw a statue with a head of gold, shoulders of silver, legs of iron, and feet of clay. These represent the kingdoms of Babylon, the Medo-Persia, the Greeks, and (the author describes) our current divided Roman kingdoms.

In Daniel's dream, he sees four animals: a lion (Babylon), a bear (Medo-Persia), a leopard (Greece), and a horrible beast—Rome. The beast had ten horns. (In Nebuchadnezzar's dream, the statue had ten toes.) Rome was broken into ten distinct kingdoms. In Daniel's dream, there was a little horn among the ten. Smith states that this is the Roman Catholic church. Three of the horns were subsequently plucked up—supposedly due to their refusal to bow to the papal authority, according to Smith. Note the quote from Smith regarding the little horn:

> **"In this horn, were eyes like the eyes of man, and a mouth speaking great things"—fit emblems of the shrewdness, penetration and arrogant claims of an apostate religious organization.**[158]

If this little horn is, in fact, the Roman Catholic church, then there must be supporting evidence. Smith obliges with countless instances of apostasy in the doctrine of the Roman Catholic church.

Christian Science

Mary Baker Eddy

Mary Baker Eddy was born Mary Baker in New England. Her father was a devout Congregationalist. Her mother was a little less zealous. The church doctrine was Calvinism. In Calvinism, your eternal destiny is already determined; there is nothing that you can do to change it. This distressed her.

Eddy was ill off and on throughout her life. Her first husband died only a year after their marriage, but not before she became pregnant. She was widowed, expecting, and had no marketable skill. She and her son lived with various relatives and friends and were often separated.

Eddy met another man and was engaged, but before they could wed, he died. She then met a dentist, Dr. Paterson. They married with the understanding that her son could not live with them. The marriage failed after several years due to alleged infidelities on his part, and her obsession with postulating the nature of health and the mind. They were divorced, and she once again was at the mercy of family and friends.

Meanwhile, she learned of a doctor named Quimby, who claimed to heal people without medicine by healing the mind. Because of her incessant ailments, she went to visit him. She did improve; however, her health was not sustained in his absence. Dr. Quimby died of cancer a year later.

She began work on her book *Science and Health* in earnest and began teaching students. In that day, anyone could take on the title of doctor with little or no medical training. Due to legislation in Massachusetts which would regulate the practice of medicine, she opened the Massachusetts School of Metaphysics—a school that taught her principles. She was the only professor, and students would get a diploma and the title of doctor after two weeks of instruction.

She later met and married Asa Gilbert Eddy, who supported her work. He was a sewing machine repairman and was the first practitioner to identify himself as a Christian Scientist on his office sign.[159] After many years of marriage, he died and she was widowed a second time.

During the course of her "work," she spoke at several churches, including Baptist churches. At two separate times she instituted her own church (chartered by Massachusetts). Her work remains as the Church of Christ, Scientist.

Science and Health

The book *Science and Health* is the companion that Eddy's devotees study along with the Bible.

I have read her book and have noted my observations here. It is difficult for me to ascertain the exact nature of Mary Baker Eddy's spiritual intent. Indeed, it is not my place to judge; however, in accordance with the challenge to test all spirits, I must make some decision as to the application of her work.

Although Eddy spends exhaustive time expounding the scripture and advocating God, Jesus, and the Holy Spirit, I find certain essential tenets missing. Namely, she does not make any mention of salvation through Jesus Christ. In fact, she makes no mention of salvation *at all*.* This may be primarily due to her Congregational foundation. She could not believe that God, who is loving and kind, would create a hell for those who offended Him. Thus, she proceeds with no explanation of any need for salvation. She reduced the word "atonement" to "at-one-ment." This is a popular device of many preachers; however, it has no basis in the word root context. In fact, the Hebrew word is *kaphar* (kaw-far) which means to cover, to expiate, to placate or cancel, cleanse, disannul, forgive, pardon or purge. By this atoning, we are then able to become *one* with God. Atonement, then, is necessary *before* we can commune with God.

While she makes arduous mention of God, she then seems to belittle the first commandment, which she interprets as:

> **Thou shalt have no belief of Life as mortal;**
> **thou shalt not know evil, for there is one**
> **Life, —even God, good.**[160]

---

* If she does make mention of salvation through Jesus, the mention was not prominent enough to remain in my memory.

Speaking of evil, she calls sin simply "error." That is, an error in thinking. If we do not think or act in accordance with how God wants us to, we are simply in error, and we need to correct that error. "Evil," she says, "has no reality."[161] She further claims that "the supposition that there are good or evil spirits, is a mistake."[162] This being the case, she sees no need for remission of sin (since there is no sin).

> **The material blood of Jesus was no more efficacious to cleanse from sin when it was shed upon "the accursed tree," than when it was flowing in his veins.**[163]

Eddy claims that the shedding of Jesus' blood did not pay for our sins. The author of Hebrews describes the Mosaic law of sacrifice in the following:

> **In fact, the law requires that nearly everything be cleansed with blood, and without the shedding of blood there is no forgiveness (Hebrews 9:22 NIV).**

Jesus Himself described the shedding of his blood this way:

> **For this is my blood of the new testament, which is shed for many *for the remission of sins* (Matthew 26:28 KJV emphasis mine).**

He was speaking, of course, about the wine at the Last Supper, which represented His actual blood which would soon be shed. What, then, does Eddy claim is the purpose of the cross?

She claims that it was for the "practical affection and goodness it demonstrated for mankind."[164]

> **Jesus suffered for our sins, not to annul the divine sentence for an individual's sin, but because sin brings inevitable suffering.**[165]

I take exception to this. I trust in Jesus because He *did* pay for my sins. Had He not paid for my sins, then I would still be under the burden of the law—to make atonement for my own sin.

Eddy makes this statement regarding Jesus:

The Millennium Agenda

> **His triumph was only because of His thorough understanding of Truth and Love.**[166]

In this passage she has actually separated Jesus from truth and love. This is significant because we see Jesus as the Son of God, that is, one with God—as being Truth and Love *incarnate*. Stating that He understood those concepts implies that He was not *inherently* those concepts.

Regarding the resurrection, Eddy claims that Jesus did rise from the dead, but only in the spirit. When pressed by the Jewish leaders to demonstrate His authority:

> **Jesus answered them, "Destroy this temple, and I will raise it again in three days" (John 2:19 NIV).**

This was a prophecy to his physical resurrection. Eddy, however, translates the verse thusly:

> **Jesus proved by his reappearance after the crucifixion in strict accordance with his scientific statement: "Destroy this temple [body], and in three days I [Spirit] will raise it up."**[167]

I am perplexed by her term "scientific statement." I do not find this to be a scientific statement, but rather a messianic statement.

Her statement indicates that the resurrection was in spirit only and not in body. This is in contradiction of the passage in Luke where Mary the mother of Jesus and the other Mary went to prepare the deceased body of Jesus.

> **On the first day of the week, very early in the morning, the women took the spices they had prepared and went to the tomb. They found the stone rolled away from the tomb, but when they entered, they did not find the body of the Lord Jesus (Luke 24:1-3 NIV).**

Furthermore, when Jesus appeared to the disciples, He presented His body to them. He still had the scars of the nails in His hand and the pierce in His side. Thomas doubted that Jesus was alive.

When Jesus appeared to him, He said:

> **"Look at my hands and my feet. It is I myself!
> Touch me and see; a ghost does not have
> flesh and bones, as you see I have."**
>
> **When he had said this, he showed them his
> hands and feet. And while they still did not
> believe it because of joy and amazement, he
> asked them, "Do you have anything here to
> eat?"**
>
> **They gave him a piece of broiled fish, and he
> took it and ate it in their presence (Luke
> 24:39-43 NIV).**

Jesus emphasized the fact that He was not a spirit (ghost) but living. He even ate food with them, not something that you would expect of a spirit.

If you think that all of Eddy's rhetoric seems to be diminishing the role of Jesus, then you are correct. In one passage she claims that Jesus is not the way (to eternal life), but the "way shower."[168]

The focus of her work is on healing—specifically, on mental healing. Medical science has shown that one's attitude about his or her recovery from illness has a big impact on the chance of recovery. The release of endorphins in the brain associated with laughter and smiling have a profound effect on health. Mary Baker Eddy did not have this information, and thus based her "science" on the same tenets in ignorance.

Unfortunately, neither she nor anyone else of that day had any idea of the physiological workings behind the teachings.

As for the word "science," Eddy uses it (or misuses it) to mean religion. In the mid and late 19th century, one could simply call oneself "doctor" and perform medicine. Similarly, Eddy used the term *science* to lend more credence to her *religion*.

I wondered as I read her biography whether she could be a true or false prophet(ess). From reading her theology in *Science and*

The Millennium Agenda

Health, I concluded that she was definitely not on the right track. Also, judging from her popularity and the lack of a salvation message, I am inclined to believe that she was a false prophet.

Her book is especially misleading because she walks the line so close to truth that the distinction is almost imperceptible. She constantly uses biblical quotes, although not always in context. She also fails to cite the reference. Note the following statement by Eddy:

> **The moral law, which has the right to acquit or condemn, always demands restitution before mortals can "go up higher."**[169]

The implication is that "go up higher" is a biblical reference. The following is the only verse in the Bible that contains the words "go up higher" in that order:

> **But when thou art bidden, go and sit down in the lowest room; that when he that bade thee cometh, he may say unto thee, Friend, *go up higher*: then shalt thou have worship in the presence of them that sit at meat with thee (Luke 14:10 KJV emphasis added).**

The King James verbiage is somewhat difficult to comprehend out of context. The *New International Version* states the same verse this way:

> **But when you are invited, take the lowest place, so that when your host comes, he will say to you, "Friend, move up to a better place." Then you will be honored in the presence of all your fellow guests (Luke 14:10 NIV).**

Jesus was telling a proverb of humility. In the proverb, Jesus admonishes all to seek the lowest place at a banquet; if the host invites you to a *higher* seat, you will then be honored. However, if you seat yourself in a *high* seat, and the host invites another to take your seat, you will be embarrassed. The next verse concludes the thought:

> **For everyone who exalts himself will be**

> **humbled, and he who humbles himself will
> be exalted (Luke 14:11 NIV).**

From this it is clear that the reference that Eddy used, although from the Bible, has nothing to do with *her* context. In fact, her use of the phrase is akin to the word "ascension" in New Age vernacular.

Rosicrucianism

In my studies of New Age influences, I frequently encountered references to the order of the Rose-Cross, or Rosicrucianism. This frequency intrigued me. I had never really looked into the Rosicrucians, or even thought much about them in light of the New Age. Curious about this connection, I looked for a Rosicrucian book that would help explain some of the basic tenets of the Rosicrucian belief structure. In so doing, I came across the book *The Rosicrucian Cosmo-Conception.* The subtitle of the book, *or Mystic Christianity*, caught my eye. I did not know that there was such a thing as "mystic Christianity."

The author of the book is Max Heindel. I suspected that it was an occult book (which was not a difficult conclusion based on the subtitle). There is a poem in the first few pages of the book titled *Creed or Christ.* The poem doesn't make a whole lot of sense, but closes out with the following lines:

> **There's but one thing the world has need to
> know,
> There's but one balm for all our human woe;
> There's but one way that leads to heaven
> above—
> That way is humane sympathy and love.**
>

Max Heindel[170]

While it is terribly tempting to tear into his philosophy (or theology) at this point, I will restrain and suffice it to say that the poem mentions Christ only in the title and does not mention Jesus at all.

The Millennium Agenda

The Rosicrucian Doctrine

The Rosicrucian doctrine as dictated by Max Heindel is based on Christianity. From my reading, it is only based on Christianity by name. The references to Jesus are few. There are more references to "Christ."

The reader is entreated to abandon former knowledge—including Christian doctrine—in order to understand Rosicrucianism. Heindel claims that all humanity desires to know the answers to these three questions:

*   Where do we come from?
*   Why are we here?
*   Where do we go after death?

Indeed, each human will ponder these questions at one time or another. Heindel claims that the only way to satisfy this longing is by a balance of knowledge of physical and "spiritual" matters.

Rosicrucianism espouses evolution. In fact, Heindel claims that wine is an essential element of our current "epoch" of evolutionary evolution. There are, Heindel claims, four prior epochs of evolution:

*   The Polarian epoch
*   The Hyperborean epoch
*   The Lemurian epoch
*   The Atlantean epoch

The current epoch, he claims, is the Aryan Epoch. (I find it interesting how the "Aryan" age [epoch] continues to surface even in different New Age philosophies.)

Mythology tells us that wine was introduced to mankind by the god Bacchus.* Heindel says that this occured in order to "numb"

---

* Bacchus, also know as Dionysus, is the Greek god of vegetation and ecstasy. He is most commonly known as the god of wine.

mankind to the knowledge that it could attain a higher state. The fact is, according to Heindel, that "it was never intended that [mankind] should go so far as that."[171]

Wine, according to Heindel, was first created by the Atlanteans:

> **After the submergence of Atlantis—a continent which once existed between Europe and America...those who escaped destruction began to cultivate the vine and make wine, as we find narrated in the Bible story of Noah. Noah symbolizes the remnant of the Atlantean Epoch, which became the nucleus of the Fifth Race—therefore our progenitors.[172]**

Heindel states that there are four kingdoms of which all matter exists: The Mineral kingdom—primarily inorganic matter; the Plant kingdom—self-explanatory; the Animal kingdom—all animals excluding humans; and the Man kingdom. The difference between each of these kingdoms is the proportion and division (in varying degrees) between the Physical World, the Desire World, the World of Thought, and Pure Spirit. Mankind is the only entity to merge all of these worlds together. In fact, the four "kingdoms" mentioned above comprise the lower four of seven worlds.

1. The World of God
2. The World of Virgin Spirits
3. The World of Divine Spirits
4. The World of Life Spirits
5. The World of Thought
6. The World of Desire
7. The Physical World

Rosicrucianism theorizes that different races are evolved differently. For instance, Heindel explains that animals feel pain differently than humans. Notice his blatant racism:

> **The feelings of animals and the lowest human races are almost entirely concerned with the gratification of the lowest desires**

The Millennium Agenda

> **and passions which find their expression in the matter of the lower Regions of the Desire World.**[173]

Heindel claims that the body has a number of "sense centers," and their range extends in spiraling patterns from various points on the body about 16 inches outward from the body. This is interesting in that it has a striking resemblance to the Hindu chakras—points of focus in the human body through which energy can be channeled for differing physiological and spiritual effects. Recall the section on crystals in Chapter 8 in this book in which an author refers to "subtle bodies" which are analogous to Heindel's "worlds" mentioned above.

Rosicrucianism espouses reincarnation and Karma, however, it cautiously avoids using these patently Hindu terms. Rather, it uses the terms:

> **Rebirth, together with its companion law, the law of consequence.**[174]

Heindel's description of these terms is essentially the same. "Rebirth" and "consequence," he explains, is the answer to why we are here, where we came from, and where we are going. He further adds:

> **The Theory of Rebirth teaches that each soul is an integral part of God, enfolding all divine possibilities as the seed enfolds the plant; that by means of repeated existences in an earthly body of gradually improving quality, the latent possibilities are slowly developed into dynamic powers; that none are lost by this process, but that all mankind will ultimately attain the goal of perfection and re-union with God.**[175]

Heindel does not give any biblical reference for this, and for good reason—there is none. He has superimposed the Hindu religion onto Christianity, and it just doesn't fit. He further makes the claim that:

> ***By the direct Command of Christ Himself*...these two laws have not been**

publicly **taught.**[176]

Again, he neglects to give any specific basis for his claim.

In fact, he claims that all religions are roads to Christianity and that they are "Race Religions and contain only in part that which Christianity has in fuller measure."[177]

Heindel has an interesting explanation for the function of blood in the human body. He claims that up to the age of fourteen, the pre-adolescent does not create blood in the marrow and thus is utilizing blood from the mother. After that time, the blood is created entirely by the marrow, and the child, now pubescent, becomes his own ego. For the blood, asserts Heindel, is the vehicle of the ego. He claims that the temperature of the blood is the cause of various physical and emotional maladies. He goes so far as to cite ancient Norse folklore regarding the (physical) intermingling of blood between two people to qualify them as kinsmen. Finally, he states that sexual maturity and activity is driven by the blood. Not, as we now know, by hormones *in* the blood.

Later in his book Heindel mentions the pituitary gland, which "medical science knows but little about" (the book was written in 1921). This demonstrates that neither he nor modern medicine had adequate, or even accurate, knowledge of most of the things he claimed to know and write about. He mentions with great confidence several "facts" which today would be considered humorous at best.

Max Heindel

I wanted to learn a little more about Max Heindel. I figured the Internet would be a good place to start. I executed a search for "Max Heindel." I found many listings, but one Internet site listing in particular caught my eye:

Rosicrucian Philosophy in Question and Answers

Develop your personal potential and inner

The Millennium Agenda

> wisdom through the Rosicrucian home study system of metaphysics, mysticism and philosophy (NOT a religion). Also home of the Rosicrucian Egyptian Museum.

Interestingly, the description of the site seems to emphatically deny that Rosicrucianism is a religion. Many Rosicrucian sites deny that it is a religion. But in fact, it is. Heindel himself proclaims it is a religion. Rosicrucianism deals with philosophical issues,belief systems, and specifically with metaphysical topics. That makes it a religion.

The listing above had a link that led to AMAZON.COM, an Internet book and music store, that enumerated many books authored by Max Heindel. I noticed this one in particular:

H.P. Blavatsky & the Secret Doctrine
Max Heindel, et al / Paperback / Published 1991

This indicates that Heindel, like Hitler, was well versed in the satanic writings of Helena Blavatsky. And indeed, he was familiar with Blavatsky. He served as vice president of the Theosophical Society from 1904-1905. He became involved with astrology (which he believed was a key to healing) and began the Rosicrucian Society shortly after. His death in 1919 is referred to as "his transition."

But let's take another look at Heindel's *The Rosicrucian Cosmo-Conception.* I began to read it and immediately was struck with occult doctrine. Not only did the occult doctrine present itself so prominently, but boasted that its founding was based on the teachings of Jesus Himself. The very first sentence in the foreword sets the tone.

> **The founder of the Christian Religion stated an occult maxim when He said: "Whosoever shall not receive the kingdom of God as a little child shall not enter therein" (Mark X:15). All occultists recognize the far-reaching importance of this teaching of Christ,**

and endeavor to "live" it day by day.[178]

I include the biblical passage that he references for comparison:

> **Verily I say unto you, Whosoever shall not
> receive the kingdom of God as a little child,
> he shall not enter therein (Mark 10:15 KJV).**

Heindel's assertion is that Jesus was implying that a person cannot enter into a belief structure with any preconceptions. In New Age vernacular, "open your mind," or "put aside the old beliefs."

> **[The student of the occult] realizes thor-
> oughly the importance of keeping his mind
> in the fluidal (sic) state of *adaptability*
> which characterizes the little child. He
> realizes in every fibre (sic) of his being that
> "now we see through a glass, darkly."**[179]

Heindel makes a reference to scripture in passing, but does not cite his reference. This is typical also of Mary Bailey and Mary Baker Eddy—the use of scriptural snippets without reference, and out of context. Below is the scripture to which Heindel alludes:

> **For now we see through a glass, darkly; but
> then face to face: now I know in part; but
> then shall I know even as also I am known
> (I Corinthians 13:12 KJV).**

Taking this verse on its own merit, it is difficult to know exactly what thought is being conveyed. Therefore, it would be easy to construe the verse to fit whatever one wanted it to apply. Let's take the verse in context and in a more current translation:

> **Love never fails. But where there are proph-
> ecies, they will cease; where there are
> tongues, they will be stilled; where there is
> knowledge, it will pass away.**
>
> **For we know in part and we prophesy in
> part, but when perfection comes, the imper-
> fect disappears.**

The Millennium Agenda

> When I was a child, I talked like a child, I
> thought like a child, I reasoned like a child.
> When I became a man, I put childish ways
> behind me. *Now we see but a poor reflection
> as in a mirror*; then we shall see face to face.
> Now I know in part; then I shall know fully,
> even as I am fully known.
>
> And now these three remain: faith, hope and
> love. But the greatest of these is love (I
> Corinthians 13:10-13 NIV).

In this passage the apostle Paul was addressing the notoriously troublesome Corinthian church. This was a pagan city and the new Christians were having a hard time focusing on what was important. In particular, they were seeking the spiritual gifts (prophecy, speaking in tongues, etc.). Paul was emphasizing that those things were less important than Christian love, which had been neglected. The term "looking through a glass darkly" refers to looking at one's reflection. The reflection is only a poor representation of who we really are. To know who we are, we must be met, face to face.

Heindel claims that Esoteric (occult) Christianity will be the ultimate world religion. While this may be true, let it not be confused with true Christianity as taught by Jesus.

In his writings, Heindel refers to the "Grand Architect of the Universe," a term used by the Masonic lodge. He also makes reference to the "Hierarchies of Celestial Beings," a term which is used in the philosophies of Mary Bailey and Helena Blavatsky. Heindel also uses the term "Godhead" which is used in Krishna (Hindu) literature.

With respect to evolution, Heindel states that the universe is cyclical—that is, it is created (evolved) and dissolved in recurring cycles. This idea is consistent with the Hindu philosophy of the universal cycle. He states that evolution leads to each person becoming a god. He proclaims that the people living on Venus and Mercury are more advanced than humans on Earth, but not quite as advanced as persons living on the sun.

In regard to Lucifer, he states that Lucifers are a class of beings
not quite as evolved as angels, but more evolved than humans.
These Lucifers were unable to evolve without a physical brain, so
they enlightened the human race:

> **They told [man] how he could cease being
> simply the servant of external powers, and
> could become his own master and like unto
> the gods, "knowing good and evil"...[they]
> brought [mankind] the inestimable blessing
> of emancipation from outside influence and
> guidance, thereby starting him on the road
> to the evolution of his own spiritual pow-
> ers.**[180]

Heindel states that Jesus was a mere host for the Christ—that
Jesus was not Christ integral.

> **At the time Christ entered the body of Jesus,
> the latter was a disciple of highest degree,
> consequently his life spirit was well
> organized.**[181]

He claims that the invitation to "whosoever will" is a solicitation
by Jesus for all to enter into the occult. Further, salvation is not
necessary for all; in fact, he claims that vicarious salvation is for
the weak populace that is not able to attain the occult spirituality
on its own.

> **Not all are in need of salvation. Christ knew
> that there is a very large class who do not
> require salvation in this way.**[182]

Heindel claims that the stories of the Knights of the Round Table
were true and that they guarded the Holy Grail (which is said to
be the cup Jesus used at the Last Supper), the spear that pierced
Jesus' side, and the cup used to collect His blood (also called the
Holy Grail) from the wound in His side.

After reading Heindel's writings, and writings about him, it seems
apparent that he is a charlatan and his teachings are clearly not
Christian as Jesus and the apostles taught.

Section IV

Current Events and End-Time Prophecy

The Millennium Agenda

Chapter 15: The One-World Government

The objective of the antichrist, according to both the New Age and the Bible, is to set up a one-world government. This is also accompanied by a one-world church. Even though that one-world church will be the official church, it will tolerate any religion except Judaism and Christianity. The reason will be that Christianity and Judaism will both oppose the antichrist and the one-world religion. Islam will probably be supported since it, too, will oppose Judaism and Christianity.

But, back to the one-world government. We have seen over and over in history where Satan has tried to establish a single world government. From the Babylonian Empire through the "Holy Roman Empire" forward, several attempts have been made to subdue the world through military might. The governments lasted only for a couple of centuries before crumbling. Hitler is the most recent attempt that we have witnessed.

However, Satan has shifted his focus from military domination to economic domination. For instance, there have been several attempts at unification of kingdoms. The Holy Roman Empire is the most notable of the relatively modern attempts. The unification of the British states (the United Kingdom) served as a small model for successfully unifying several independent states under a single governmental structure. The United States was an even larger exercise in unifying independent states.

The original thirteen colonies were each a state. Today, we in the United States have become accustomed to thinking of states as those entities naturally subjugated to a higher federal authority. However, the first thirteen colonies did not have a federal government. They each had a sovereign (or so declared) government. They knew that they could not independently defeat the British armies, so they united in the form of the First and Second Continental Congress. Peyton Randolf was unanimously elected president *of the congress* in 1774. This act thus created the terms "president" and "congress" as we know them today.

Peyton Randolf was elected as president; that is, to preside over the congress. When he was elected, he was merely elected to act as mediator, or chairman of the congress—not as the chief official of the collective states. This is why George Washington is considered the first president of the United States. It was not until *after* the Declaration of Independence in 1776 that the thirteen states claimed the name "The United States."

The Continental Congress financed the rebellion against Britain by selling war bonds and issuing currency. Now at this time, the individual states were also issuing currency (as was their right as an independent state.)

The young states attempted on a few occasions to assemble and determine the future as independent states. In one convention, only a meager few states sent delegates. Alexander Hamilton proposed yet another convention, which would take place in Philadelphia.

> **[Hamilton] was convinced that only drastic centralization would save the nation from disintegration.**[183]

This convention, known as the Philadelphia Convention, assembled on May 25, 1787. George Washington was promptly elected president of the convention. There was still no president of the United States. Within four months, the convention had drafted the Constitution. On May 30th, the delegates voted that a national government ought to be established. They then set about to work out the details.

The first question was that of economics, demonstrating that power lies in economics.

> **The right to levy taxes and to regulate interstate and foreign commerce was assigned to the central government almost without debate.**[184]

And with equal expedience:

> **...the states were deprived of their right to issue money coin or paper...**[185]

The second item of business was to establish a common military complex.

The Millennium Agenda

If, however, the mark of an independent sovereign government is to regulate commerce, then consider the recent North American Free Trade Agreement (NAFTA):

> **1. The objectives of this Agreement, as elaborated more specifically through its principles and rules, including national treatment, most-favored nation treatment and transparency are to:**
>
> > **(a) eliminate barriers to trade in, and facilitate the cross border movement of, goods and services between the territories of the Parties;**
> >
> > **(b) promote conditions of fair competition in the free trade area;**
> >
> > **(c) increase substantially investment opportunities in their territories;**
> >
> > **(d) provide adequate and effective protection and enforcement of intellectual property rights in each Party's territory;**
> >
> > **(e) create effective procedures for the implementation and application of this Agreement, and for its joint administration and the resolution of disputes; and**
> >
> > **(f) establish a framework for further trilateral, regional and multilateral cooperation to expand and enhance the benefits of this Agreement.**
>
> **2. The Parties shall interpret and apply the provisions of this Agreement in the light of its objectives set out in paragraph 1 and in accordance with applicable rules of interna-**

tional law.[186]

In short, to have great influence over, if not complete control of, international commerce between North American countries.

Further, consider the Global Agreement for Trades and Tariffs (GATT), which has recently become the World Trade Organization (WTO).

> **GATT (the institution) was small and provisional, and not even recognized in law as an international organization. It has now been replaced by the World Trade Organization. GATT (the agreement) has been amended and incorporated into the new WTO Agreements. GATT deals only with trade in goods. The WTO Agreements now cover services and intellectual property as well.**[187]

Speaking of GATT:

> **The original intention was to create a third institution handling international economic cooperation.**[188]

The WTO further explains its objectives:

> **The agreements have three main objectives: to help trade flow as freely as possible, to achieve further liberalization gradually through negotiation, and to set up an impartial means of settling disputes.**[189]

GATT is not nearly as new as some people think. It only gained popular recognition because of President Clinton's efforts to have the United States ratify the agreement.

> **The WTO's creation in 1995 marked the biggest reform of international trade since 1948. During those 47 years, international commerce had come under GATT which helped establish a prosperous multilateral trading system. But by the 1980s an overhaul was due.**[190]

The Millennium Agenda

Again, it appears that economic control has been placed in the hands of a world organization rather than with the individual nations. I am not passing judgment on the goodness or badness of GATT or the WTO. My point is that these are both world organizations. When the economic controls pass into the hands of a world organization, then the political power is soon to follow.

Consider the creation of the Eurodollar. This currency became active January 1, 1999 and replaced eleven major currencies of Western Europe. Now that most of Western Europe has a unified currency and economic system, a unified government in Europe is the next step toward the one-world government.

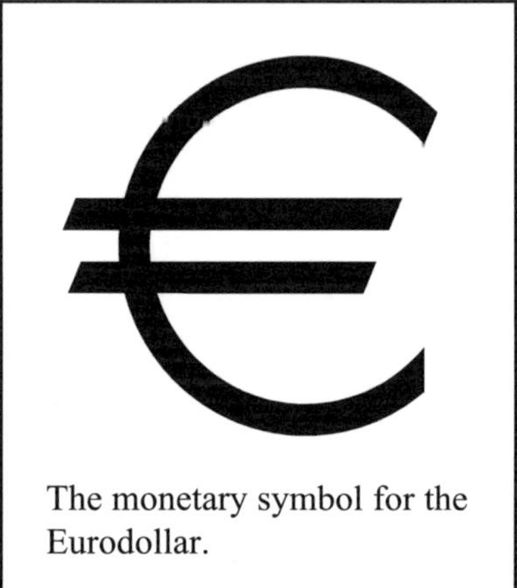

The monetary symbol for the Eurodollar.

Just as the Philadelphia congress found economic power the primary focus and military power the secondary focus, so the United Nations has established an international policing organization. In 1947, a freshman representative from California named Richard Nixon introduced House Concurrent Resolution 68, which contains the following text:

> **It is the sense of Congress that the President of the United States should immediately take the initiative in calling a General Conference of the United Nations pursuant to (U.N.) Article 109 for the purpose of making the United Nations capable of enforcing world law.**[191]

We have seen in our lifetime several examples of how the United Nations has acted as a police agency by its presence. In Korea in the early 1950s, the United States and other nations sent troops as a "police action" to assist the South Korean government. In the late 1950s through the mid 1970s, the United States and other nations sent troops to assist the South Vietnamese government. The United Nations sent forces to assist refugees in Rwanda and Zaire. The United Nations also sent forces to Serbia that took a more active role with refugees.

In numerous other situations, we have seen the United Nations make its presence. We have also seen that its presence has become more authoritative over the years. In fact, many people are now *asking* the United Nations to take a more forceful role in settling civil and international disputes.

I think that we are only a short distance from seeing the United Nations military force preempt any national military. In fact, national military organizations will slowly become only token organizations while the United Nations armed forces will act not as a defensive force, but as a massive policing agency.

One journalist questioned the United States presence in the Balkan States (Bulgaria, Albania, Greece, Romania, part of Turkey, and the countries of the former Yugoslavia). According to his article in the *Investor's Business Daily* (June 1998), there were still 10,000 troops in the Balkans. His opening statement summarizes his attitude regarding NATO and the role of the United States military force:

> **With NATO jets screaming through the skies around Kosovo, two things seem certain: The U.S. has become the world's policeman, and the Balkans are its beat.**[192]

NATO has acted as the commanding force in the Balkans; however, on the world stage the United States acts as the executive arm of the United Nations. In almost every conflict involving United Nations peacekeeping forces, the United States has played a dominant role.

My point is this: the antichrist will rise amid a global government, or some global leglislative and executive structure. The United Nations appears to be that structure, and we see that with each new conflict, the United Nations takes on less of an arbitrator role, and more of a governing role. Just as we lay a massive foundation for a skyscraper, we also seem to have laid out a suitable foundation for a world government in the form of the United Nations.

Chapter 16: The Next Stage

We know several things regarding the last days from the writings of Daniel and The Revelation. In particular, we know that there will have been four major kingdoms of this world.

Recall Daniel's interpretation of Nebuchadnezzar's dream of the statue which had a head of gold, chest of silver, thighs of brass, legs of iron, and feet of iron and clay. The first of these, the head of gold, is believed to be the Babylonian kingdom, the first and most glorious of the "world" kingdoms. That empire would soon give way to the Medo-Persian Empire, the chest of silver.

This would be followed by the Greek rule (thighs of brass) and the Roman empire (legs of iron). Of particular interest is that the feet have ten toes. This was significant in the king's dream and represented the division that was to occur following the collapse of the Roman Empire.

Further, what we know is that the kingdom of the antichrist will be amid a coalition of ten kings. This can be presumed to be representatives of each of the ten divisions of the Roman Empire.

I have a more general interpretation.

Many suspect, and I believe it to be true, that the real political forces of this world are driven by economics. That is, the real kings of this world are the persons who hold such immeasurable wealth that they can "buy" not only politicians, but entire government cabinets. (By the way, Bill Gates is considered a small time player among these ranks.)

The number of these individuals or families is approximately ten (depending on your criteria). In my research, I have read several books whose authors name individuals or families they believe to be among these ten. The authors' investigations reveal some fascinating facts about their roles in end-time prophecy.

The Millennium Agenda

The Hapsburg Dynasty

The family that tops my list is the Hapsburg family (also spelled Habsburg). This family has the distinction of being the oldest living and still recognized ruling family in Europe. The Hapsburgs ruled in Europe for hundreds of years (1282–1918). In 1867 the empire which was ruled by the Hapsburg dynasty became the Austro-Hungarian monarchy. This monarchy was dissolved at the end of World War I. Hitler invaded Austria in World War II. The Hapsburgs remain and retain their title yet do not act in the (public) political arena.

One of the reasons that Hitler wanted to capture Austria was that there was a relic in Austria believed to be the spear that pierced Jesus' side while He hung on the cross. Hitler did capture the relic, but it was returned to Austria after the war.

This begs the question: "Why would Hitler be interested in the spear that pierced Jesus?" For the same reason that he pursued the Ark of the Covenant and the Holy Grail. Hitler read and believed the writings of Helena Blavatsky. Among other things, she claims that mystical powers can inhabit certain objects. Jesus, according to Blavatsky, had captured so much of this mystical power that even objects that had touched Him were imbued with excessive power. This power, it is assumed, can be harnessed and used to control the matter and circumstances.

Hitler believed that many of these relics held mystical power and if he could obtain them—and control them—he could become the central world ruler; a god, if you will.

In the ninth chapter of Matthew, we have the story of the woman with an aneurism. She believed that if she touched His clothing that she would be healed. Blavatsky would argue that this displays the magical properties that inhabited even Jesus' clothing. But, note that Jesus corrected the woman by telling her that it was her faith, not His garment, that had healed her. Jesus wanted to be clear that faith was what we should consider to be important, not things. Jesus never used crystals, wands, or any other physical device in His miracles. He demonstrated to us how to use faith.

But, back to the Hapsburgs. Many people believed (and some still believe) that the possession of this relic is the reason for the continuing endurance of the Hapsburg dynasty. The Hapsburgs are linked to the Lorraines, a ruling dynasty of France, and the Lorraines are linked to the Merovingians who claim to be descendants of Jesus. It is believed that the spear was passed to the Hapsburgs through this supposed bloodline from Jesus.

It is apparent that the Hapsburgs still hold to this supposed bloodline since the current eldest Hapsburg, Otto von Habsburg, claims as his titles Archduke of Austria and King of Jerusalem.

Other Candidates

Other persons who have been identified, not necessarily as the antichrist, but as members of an elite ruling body, include the following:

- King Don Juan Carlos of Spain who claims to be a descendant of Jesus and claims the title King of Jerusalem.
- The Bronfman Dynasty - enormously wealthy and members of several international organizations (whose purposes are the betterment of humankind).
- The Oppenheimer Dynasty - diamond moguls.
- The Rothschild Dynasty - European banking family with Jewish roots, notable for huge international loans.
- The Rockefeller Dynasty - industry and banking moguls in the U.S. Donated site for U.N. building in New York. Also founded the Trilateral Commission.
- The British Royal Family - one of the few remaining ruling monarchy families of the world and the most recognized among Europe.

While it is not my intention to assert or imply any particular individual as the antichrist, I do want to point out that there is a group of families who are keenly interested in international affairs and literally have the means to economically sway political interests to suit their desires.

The politicians that we supposedly elect may very well be chosen and placed in power by the influence, or dare we say, craftiness of these families.

The group of ten individuals or families (which may or may not comprise any of those mentioned above), is known as the Illuminati. While the exact nature and membership of this group is not known, it is said to be an inner circle of ten men who are the real political force in this world.

The Overseers

 The trademark of the Illuminati is probably best illustrated by the symbol on the reverse side of the United States one dollar bill. This emblem, entitled the Great Seal, shows a pyramid with the capstone raised above the peak and an eye peering over the scene.

Across the bottom of the seal is the phrase "NOVUS ORDO SECLORUM," which literally means "New World Order."

The words across the top are "ANNUIT COEPTIS." I was unable to get a translation of this phrase because I could not get a fix on the language that was used. According to the U.S. Treasury, the phrase translates as "He (God) has favored our undertakings," claiming to make reference to the divine providence during our government's formation.[193]

The inscription at the base of the pyramid is the Roman Numeral representation of 1776 (MDCCLXXVI), the year of proclaimed independence.

The "Great Seal" was added to U.S. currency in the 1930s.

One explanation of the unfinished pyramid and eye is that the unfinished pyramid demonstrates that the United States will constantly be building or changing—never "finished." The eye, according to the U.S. Treasury, is the Eye of Providence (God).

A less popular interpretation of the symbol is that the pyramid represents the classes of society and the eye, which appears illuminated and raised above the rest of the pyramid, is the elite ruling class which has the divine authority to oversee the rest of the classes.

I will let you decide which explanation you find more plausible. But before you decide, consider how the symbolism fits into the New Age plan and remember that the New Age will use the terms for God and "divine guidance" much differently than mainstream Christianity. Also, generic terms for God, like "divine providence," are common among Masonic literature and ritual.

Ten Kings

We know from the books of Daniel and The Revelation that there will be ten kings (rulers) that rise in the time of the antichrist.

> **And the ten horns which thou sawest are ten kings, which have received no kingdom as yet; but receive power as kings one hour with the beast.**
>
> **These have one mind, and shall give their power and strength unto the beast (Revelation 17:12-13 KJV).**

Kings that have no kingdom would be an adequate description of the Illuminati. They have "one mind" as if to imply that they have the same objective. From among these ten kings will rise the antichrist.

We also know that three of the kings will be removed. I take from this that the three that are removed will be good for political acceptance, but once control is gained, the three will be cast aside with no more usefulness.

> **I considered the horns, and, behold, there came up among them another little horn,**

**before whom there were three of the first
horns plucked up by the roots: and, behold,
in this horn were eyes like the eyes of man,
and a mouth speaking great things (Daniel
7:8 KJV).**

This is a model of the Temple in Jerusalem that was built by Herod. Herod was a vain man and wanted to outdo all of his contemporaries and thus is responsible for several magnificent architechtural marvels in Israel.

The Big Sellout

We also know that the antichrist will have a religious sidekick. I believe this to be a major Christian denomination with worldwide visibility. At this time, the Roman Catholic church would meet that criteria.

First, I believe this to be a religious figure because the antichrist will be a political figure and will need some religious figure to point to him as the solver of the world's problems. Secondly, I believe this will be a representative of a Christian denomination because all New Age and other religions will welcome the antichrist unwittingly. Even Judaism will accept the antichrist because he will appear to be the Messiah.

How can the antichrist be perceived as the Messiah? He will be of Hebrew descent (or Jewish, at least). He will come on the world scene to bring peace to Israel. Indeed, the primary agenda of the antichrist will be to make a peace treaty with Israel. (Everything that I have read concerning the antichrist implies that the antichrist will not be from Israel.) I believe, however, that the antichrist will be set up as a leader (Prime Minister or some other principal role) within Israel and will make treaties with the historic enemies of Israel. In this way, Israel can be sabotaged from within.

The importance of the treaty is that currently, the old city of Jerusalem is divided into four quarters. The temple mound lies

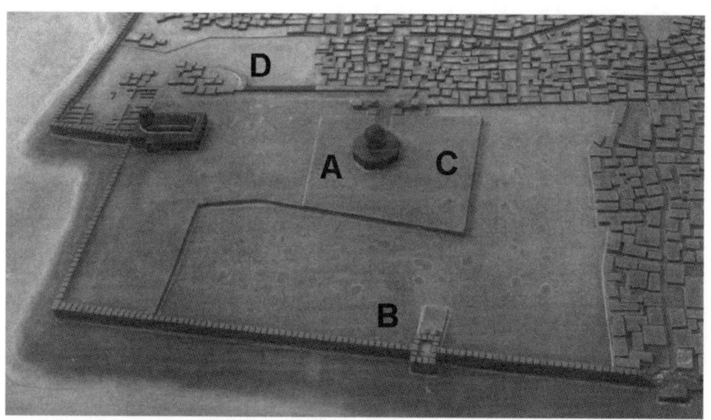

This is a layout of the current city of Jerusalem. The letter "A" indicates the Dome of the Rock. The letter "B" is the Eastern Gate. The letter "C" is the presumed location of the Holy of Holies in the original temple and thus the site of the new temple. The letter "D" is Western Wall of the old city and now the site of the former "Wailing Wall." I was informed that the wall is now called the "Wall of Rejoicing" in anticipation of the Messiah who will reclaim the temple.

within the Arab controlled area. We are told in the Bible that the antichrist will build a temple in Jerusalem on the site of the temple in Jesus' time (Solomon's temple). In order for a Jewish temple to be built on the Temple mound, a treaty is essential. The treaty will be established with the Arab nations and construction will begin on the temple. Once it is complete, the treaty will fail but the antichrist will remain. He will set up his throne in the temple, botray the Jews, but retain the throne in the temple.

Back to the religious sidekick. Revelation speaks of the sidekick:

> **And there came one of the seven angels
> which had the seven vials, and talked with
> me, saying unto me, Come hither; I will show
> unto thee the judgment of the great whore
> that sitteth upon many waters: With whom
> the kings of the earth have committed forni-
> cation, and the inhabitants of the earth have
> been made drunk with the wine of her
> fornication (Revelation 17:1-2 KJV).**

I find the imagery of a whore particularly significant in that it is one who has sold his or her virtue for worldly gratification. Also contrast this with the "bride" of Christ. This bride, represented by a virginal maiden, waits for her husband to come and get her.

If, for instance, the maiden tires of waiting or decides to follow her own interests, she defiles herself before her husband. She becomes a shame and a disgrace to him.

In this way, only a Christian denomination could defile Christ.

Further, we are told that the whore has defiled herself with the kings of the world. This tells me that this Christian representative has "sold-out" to the purposes of the kings of this world and to their objectives rather than the purposes of Christ. And, if she compromises the gospel which has been entrusted to her, she "intoxicates" the whole world into believing that which is not true and ignoring the truth.

> **And he saith unto me, The waters which**

> **thou sawest, where the whore sitteth, are
> peoples, and multitudes, and nations, and
> tongues (Revelation 17:15 KJV).**

This demonstrates the reach of the apostate Christian
denomination. Many nations and languages will represent it. I
believe this apostate Christian denomination to be the Roman
Catholic church. The sidekick, in particular, will be the active
pope at the time.

The angel shows John more about the woman.

> **And I saw the woman drunken with the
> blood of the saints, and with the blood of the
> martyrs of Jesus: and when I saw her, I
> wondered with great admiration (Revelation
> 17:6 KJV).**

Is the Catholic church guilty of murdering saints and martyrs?
Consider the Crusades and the Inquisition.

John witnesses the fate of the woman:

> **And the ten horns which thou sawest upon
> the beast, these shall hate the whore, and
> shall make her desolate and naked, and shall
> eat her flesh, and burn her with fire (Revela-
> tion 17:16 KJV).**

The ten kings will destroy the Catholic church when they have
gained what they wanted from it.

What to Expect

In the coming years and decades, we will experience the greatest
attack on the gospels that has ever occurred.

The New Age teaches and will teach with stronger emphasis that
all roads lead to heaven. Evangelism is a violation of an
individual's religious disposition. And any religion (like
Christianity) that does not "tolerate" the others should be
eliminated, even with violence, if necessary.

The Millennium Agenda

There will be increased portrayal of witchcraft and occult activities as normal in the television and movie industry. This will include paranormal (ghost) and alien portrayals.

The world government will institute a new worldwide economic order in which a single worldwide currency will replace national currencies. And eventually, electronic commerce will replace currency altogether. We will become a cashless society.

The United Nations will abolish all individual national armies and all military institutions will become U.N. peacekeeping forces. A worldwide tax will be instituted to distribute wealth to poorer nations. The groundwork for this was laid by ratification of GATT, now the World Trade Organization.

New Age religions will be mandatory in schools, but Christianity will be prohibited. These New Age religions will not be taught as religion, but as thought processes, or mental stimulation. Prayers will become mandatory, but will be New Age prayers. Meditation and other New Age techniques will become common curriculum. Institutional prayers will become commonplace but will be edited by the instution, or dictated and uniform like the Great Invocation, a New Age prayer written by Alice Bailey.

Guns will be banned. They will be blamed for the excess of crime and thus will be removed from the hands of responsible citizens.

The Catholic church—in particular, the Pope—will become more visible in world political events. Versions of the Bible will compromise the gospel: gender neutral versions, for example, will lead this transformation. Minor changes in the translations will begin to distort the Gospels as we know them.

A new temple will be built in Jerusalem and Jewish activity worldwide will become more commonplace.

The "Christ" will be portrayed not as a mighty omnipotent God, but rather as an enlightened "master."

Stand Firm

As a Christian in the last days, it will become more important for you to be sure of your doctrine and to guard against false teachings. Paul repeatedly warned against false teachers and false doctrines. It almost seems as if he was addressing our age.

Your Christian practices will be called into question and you will be required to clearly state where you stand.

> **Put on the full armor of God so that you can take your stand against the devil's schemes. For our struggle is not against flesh and blood, but against the rulers, against the authorities, against the powers of this dark world and against the spiritual forces of evil in the heavenly realms.**
>
> **Therefore put on the full armor of God, so that when the day of evil comes, you may be able to stand your ground, and after you have done everything, to stand (Ephesians 6:11-13 NIV).**

Let me encourage you. Even though this all seems like a discouraging outlook on our future, take heart; these are also the signs that our God is coming soon! This may be the generation that experiences, firsthand, the glorious return of our Lord Jesus Christ.

The Millennium Agenda

Glossary

Age of Aquarius: The race [or generation] of people who realize that they are capable of achieving god-hood.

Animism: The belief in myriad spirit beings who are concerned with human affairs and are capable of helping or harming people's interests. Also, the belief that spirits can inhabit inanimate objects.

Aryan Race: This is the evolutionary state in which mankind achieves god-hood.

Brahman: The Hindu concept of god in which all creation is merely a dream, the dream of Brahman. And when Brahman stops dreaming, then all creation, as we know it, ceases to be.

Crystals: Crystals are capable of releasing energy when some form of stress is placed upon them. This is the motive force in the quartz watch. However, New Agers believe that holding crystals in the hand, or placing them on strategic parts of the body, can bring about healing, rejuvenation or wisdom.

Dimension: The particular usage of this word may suggest its New Age meaning. Any usage dealing with another dimension (as in traveling to another dimension) is particularly New Age. New Age doctrine teaches that man can transcend the dimensions as we now know them. In fact, many angels and aliens (actually demons) who contact people claim to be from another dimension.

Diversity: This term is used most commonly in the workplace as a phrase to describe tolerance (ethnic, gender, religious, sexual preference, etc.).

Divination: The term "divining rod" may be more familiar. The divining rod was used to find water. Divination is the practice of using some inanimate object to "divine" an answer.

Enlightened, Enlightenment, Illumined: These terms were originally associated with Hinduism. A person who has been *enlightened* has reached an elevated evolutionary state (in some cases, has reached god-hood).

Ether: Physical matter, not homogeneous matter, but something comprising spirit and matter. This ether controls such aspects as gender and warm- or cold-bloodedness. Ghosts and angels are supposedly composed of ether.

Gnosticism: A religious and philosophical belief structure that thrived around the very early Christian era and was (and is) heretical. Its fundamental principle is that salvation comes through knowledge (gnosis) rather than through faith or religious works. That knowledge is not knowledge of who God is, but the knowledge that one may rise to a state of god-hood.

God of Nature: This is a cryptic reference to earth worship. The meaning is actually "the god *consisting of* nature." This term is frequently used by New Agers and in public prayers. It does not refer to Jehovah God.

Holistic: A method of utilizing all natural foods and elements to effect health and healing. It is usually associated with crystals and other "natural" substances that are not classified as drugs by the FDA. Holistic healing is frequently used in conjunction with occult practices such as divination and spiritism.

Jainism: The form of Hinduism that forbids injury to any living creature.

Life Force, Energy: These terms refer to nature as god. The life force is what causes all things to be. This belief supersedes any belief in a divine creator.

Love and Light: This phrase is frequently embedded in New Age propaganda. It does not refer to the Christian idea of light (Christ), but of knowledge or enlightenment. **Light** is a common theme in New Age philosophy. Angels, aliens, and apparitions are often shrouded in "light" or speak of light. Persons who claim to have died and come back to life speak of being consumed by light. Books such as *Dancing in the Light, Embraced by the Light, Closer to the Light, Transformed by the Light* and others lead the reader to occult, New Age philosophies.

Mother Earth, Planet Earth: These terms are usually associated with persons or groups which, in effect, worship the earth.

Necromancy: This term is generally thought to mean a form of magic; however; its meaning is far more sinister than that. *Necr* is Latin for the dead (generally a cadaver). The full word indicates a form of magic specifically involving seances and other summoning.

New Age, New World Order, The Plan: These phrases refer to the coming order, the next evolutionary state of mankind as a whole. In Christian terms, this refers to the unholy one world government spoken of in the end times. President George Bush used the term "New World Order" frequently in his addresses.

The Millennium Agenda

Nirvana: This is defined as the ultimate existence that transcends suffering, specifically sought in Buddhism through the elimination of desire and individual consciousness. This word has become commonplace in our society as (mistakenly) meaning a state of happiness.

Reason: A cryptic code word meaning the worship of Lucifer through self-deification.

Religion: The New Age describes religion as a noble endeavor in which its participants subscribe to a given set of morals and disciplines for the purpose of self-realization [self-deification].

Spirit Guide: In New Age terms, a person who helps guide one through spiritual growth—otherwise known as a medium.

Spiritism: The practice of summoning spirits. The most common form of spiritism in practice today is Shamanism, the Native American religious activities of consulting the dead for advice and guidance.

Synchronicity: This term is used to give personality and intelligence to nature to account for apparent coincidental events. Occultists use these coincidental events to validate their activities. In Christian terms, we speak of the working of the Holy Spirit to guide us. In the same way, demonic forces can guide people away from truth. People who do not wish to acknowledge either a god or demons call this synchronicity.

Theosophy: The satanic religion that encompasses the principles for the New Age and for the foundation of the one-world government, popularized by Helena Blavatsky's book *The Secret Doctrine*, a favorite of Hitler and others who wish to dominate the world.

Wicca: the arcane name for witchcraft.

Index

A

A Course in Miracles 101
Age of Aquarius 107
Aliens 61, 72, 199
    at the movies 68
    NASA 64
    UFO's 10
    Val Thor 67
Anderson, George 89
Angels
    angel contact 56
    evil 58
    Genesis, Chapter 6 27
    holy 57
    Introduction 11
    Islam 23
    New Age stories 56
    of light 13, 72, 91
    seraphim and cherubim 59
Animism 18
Antichrist 129, 130, 186
Apollonius 126, 127, 128
Aura 79
Automatic Writing 24

B

Bailey, Alice A. 120
Blavatsky, Helena
        49, 110, 114, 120, 203
Buddhism 20

C

Candles 81

Carbon Dating 46
Cartoons
    Introduction 11
Celestine Prophecy 106
Chakras 79
Channeling 87
Chariots of the Gods 66
Cherubim 59
Christ 9
Christian Science 156
Collectivism 51
Computer games 11
Confucianism 21
Crystals 75, 78, 81

D

Darwin, Charles 42
DeMolay
    Jacques 139
    order 139
Diversity 10
Dome of the Rock 187
Dowling, Levi H. 107

E

Eadie, Betty 83
Eastern Star 138
Eddy, Mary Baker 156
Eldredge, Niles 45
Embraced by The Light 83
Energy 18
Environmental Responsibility 37
Environmentalism 37

The Millennium Agenda

Evolution 42, 49
   carbon dating 46
   Darwin, Charles 42
   Eldredge, Niles 45
   Gould, Stephen Jay 45

G

Global Peace 39
Gnosticism 18
God 9
Gothic Subcultures 75
Gould, Stephen Jay 45

H

Hapsburg Dynasty 182
Hegel, Georg Wilhelm Friedrich 50
Hiearchy 24
Hiendel, Max 167
Hinduism 19
Holy Grail 144

I

Illuminati 184, 185
Isis Temple
   Masonic lodge 138
Islam 23

J

Jesus 9
   claims of deity 131
   second coming 133
Joseph of Arimathea 143
Judge, William Quan 113

K

Kant, Immanuel 50
Karma 19
Knights Templar 140, 142

L

Light 13
Lucifer 65, 123

M

Maitreya 121, 129, 198
Mars 62
Martial Arts 24
Mary Magdalene 143
Masters 24
Meditation 10
Merovingians 145, 147
Monism 18
Monotheism 18
Moral Relativism 40, 50
Morals 9
   moral absolute 9

N

NASA 64
Nature 10
NDE. *See* Near Death Experience
Near Death Experience 13, 83
Necromancy 77
Nirvana 10

O

Olcott, Henry S. 113
One-World Government 174
Order and Purpose 72
Order of Freemasons
   Masonic Lodge 137
Order of the Eastern Star 138
Origin of Species 42
Osiris Temple
   Masonic lodge 138
Ouija Board
   occult activities 77

Ouroboros 110

P

Paganism 75
Pantheism 18
Planetary Hierarchy 24
Polytheism 18
Prayer
  New Age 10
Priori de Sion 142
Psychic Medium
    channeling 87
    witchcraft 77
Punctuated Equilibrium 45
Pyramids 66
Pythagoras 127

R

Redfield, James 106
Reincarnation 19
Relative Evil 40, 50
Religion 10
    alien contact 71
Roman Catholic Church 150
Rosicrucianism 163

S

Sagan, Carl 61
Satan 65
Schucman, Dr. Helen 101
Scottish Rite, The 138
Secret Organizations 137
Self Discovery 38
Seraphim 59
Shinto 22
Shriners, The 138
Silva Mind Control 15
Sin 9
    near death experiences 86

Socialism 51
Socorro, New Mexico 62
Solovyov, Vsevolod Sergueyevich
    111
Sorcery 77
Spiritism
    witchcraft 78
Star Trek 69

T

Taoism 20
Temple Mound 187
Theosophy
    111, 114, 115, 116, 117, 118, 120
Transmission Meditation 24

U

UFO Abduction 64

V

Visualization 15
Von Däniken, Erich 66
Voodoo 78

W

Western Wall 187
Wicca 75
Witches 75

Y

Yin Yang 15, 21

Endnotes

[1] Ross, Hugh, Ph.D. <u>The Creator and the Cosmos</u>. Colorado Springs, Colorado, Navpress. 1993. p105.

[2] Lalonde, Peter and Paul. <u>2000 A.D. Are You Ready?</u> Nashville, Thomas Nelson Publishers. 1997. p87.

[3] Jeremiah, David, and C.C Carlson. <u>Invasion of Other Gods</u>. Dallas: Word Publishing, 1995.

[4] Share International Internet site: http://www.shareintl.org/ transmission.html. Maitreya: Transmission Meditation. 1998. No copyright posted.

[5] <u>Biblical Archaeology Review</u>. Volume 21, Number 5. September/ October 1995. Cover photo by Richard Nowitz.

[6] Hirschfeld, Yizhar, "Spirituality in the Desert: Judean Wilderness Monasteries," <u>Biblical Archaeology Review</u>, Volume 21, Number 5. September/October 1995. p.29

[7] ibid. Hirschfeld, p.30.

[8] Freedman, David Noel, and Jeffrey C. Geoghegan, "'House of David' Is There!," <u>Biblical Archaeology Review</u>, Volume 21, Number 2. March/April 1995. p.78.

[9] Rainey, Anson F. "Queries & Comments," <u>Biblical Archaeology Review</u>, Volume 21, Number 5. September/October 1995. p.20.

[10] Gish, Duane T., Ph.D., <u>Evolution: The Challenge of the Fossil Record</u>. El Cajon, California, Creation-Life Publishers. 1986.

[11] Ross, Hugh, Ph.D. <u>The Creator and the Cosmos</u>. Colorado Springs, Colorado. Navpress. 1993.

[12] Ross, ibid.

[13] Gish, ibid.

[14] Discoveries: The Dallas Morning News. Monday, October 19, 1998.

[15] Whitehead, John W. <u>The Stealing of America</u>. Westchester, Illinois. Crossway Books. 1983.

[16] Banes, N. H., ed. <u>The Speeches of Adolf Hitler</u>. London. Oxford Press. 1942.

[17] Whitehead, ibid.

[18] Doe, Mimi Walch, "A Word About Angels" Internet site: http://www.intouchmag.com/mimi.html . 1998. Copyright 1996.

[19] Doe, ibid.

[20] Doe, ibid.

[21] Doe, ibid.

[22] Doe, ibid.

[23] Lemke, Steve. "Angels and the Angel" <u>Biblical Illustrator</u>. Spring 1990, p20.

[24] Moore, Patrick. <u>Travellers in Space and Time</u>. London, Doubleday & Company. 1983.

[25] Sagan, Carl. <u>Cosmos</u>. New York, Random House. 1980. p.288.

[26] ibid. p.261. photo Bill Ray.

[27] Evans, Hilary. <u>UFOs: The Greatest Mystery</u>. London, Albany Books. 1979.

[28] Begley, Sharon. "Mission to Mars," *Newsweek*, September 23, 1996 ©1996 Newsweek, Inc. all rights reserved. Reprinted by permission. Pp. 52 - 58

[29] Begley, ibid.

[30] Internet site: http://www.nrao.edu/vla/html/VLAintro.shtml ; National Radio Astronomy Observatory and Associated Universities, Inc. Photos and text used by permission.

[31] *The American Heritage® Dictionary of the English Language, Third Edition* copyright © 1992 by Houghton Mifflin Company. Electronic version licensed from InfoSoft International, Inc. All rights reserved.

[32] Internet site: http://abduct.com/terminol.htm . Copyright © 1997 Alien Abduction Experience and Research.

[33] Alnor, William N. <u>UFOs in the New Age: extraterrestrial messages and the truth of Scripture</u>. Grand Rapids, Michigan, Baker Books. 1992.

[34] Von Däniken, Erich. <u>Chariots of the Gods? Memories of the Future—and Unsolved Mysteries of the Past.</u> Translated by Michael Heron, New York, G. P. Putnam's Sons. 1968.

[35] Alnor, ibid.

[36] Alnor, ibid.

[37] Casson, Lionel, et al. <u>Mysteries of the Past</u>. New York, American Heritage Publishing Co. ©1977.

[38] Stranges, Frank E. PhD. <u>The Stranger at the Pentagon</u>. Van Nuys, California, I.E.C., Inc. Book Division. ©1967.

[39] Stranges, ibid.

[40] Lalonde, ibid. p52.

[41] Lalonde, ibid. p53.

[42] Lalonde, ibid. p56.

[43] Lalonde, ibid. p56.

[44] Clarke, Robert B. publisher. <u>The Supernatural; Visitors From Outer Space</u>. London, Aldus Books Limited. ©1976. P75.

[45] Praagh, James Van. <u>Talking To Heaven: A Medium's Message Of Life After Death</u>. Copyright © 1997 by James Van Praagh. Used by Permission of Dutton, a division of Penguin Putnam Inc.

[46] Bowman, Catherine. Crystal Ascension. St. Paul, Minnesota. Llewellyn Publications. ©1996. p.37.

[47] Bowman, ibid. p.5.

[48] Bowman, ibid. p.7.

[49] Bowman, ibid. p.8.

[50] Bowman, ibid. p.30.

[51] Bowman, ibid. p.33.

[52] Bowman, ibid. p.159.

[53] Crystals of the Light Internet site: <u>http://www.wwwcomm.com/ crystals/index.html</u> . 1998. No copyright posted.

[54] Crystals of the Light , ibid.

[55] Crystals of the Light , ibid.

[56] Eadie, Betty J. <u>Embraced by the Light.</u> Carson City, Nevada. Gold Leaf Press. ©1992. p113.

[57] Eadie, ibid. p114.

[58] Eadie, ibid. p85.

[59] Eadie, ibid. p45.

[60] Eadie, ibid. p109.

[61] Eadie, ibid. p47.

[62] Eadie, ibid. p48.

[63] Eadie, ibid. p84.

[64] Eadie, ibid. p49.

[65] Eadie, ibid. p69.

[66] Groothius, Doug. <u>Deceived by the Light</u>. Eugene, Oregon. Harvest House Publishers. ©1995.

[67] Praagh, ibid. p67.

[68] Praagh, ibid. p56.

[69] Praagh, ibid. p62.

[70] Praagh, ibid. p103.

[71] Praagh, ibid. p69.

[72] Praagh, ibid. p83.

[73] Praagh, ibid. p84.

[74] Praagh, ibid. p84.

[75] Martin, Joel and Patricia Romanowski. <u>We Don't Die: George Anderson's Conversations With The Other Side</u>. Copyright © 1988 by Joel Martin PAR Bookworks, Ltd. Used by permission of Putnam Berkley, a division of Penguin Putnam Inc. p33.

[76] Martin, ibid. p37.

[77] Martin, ibid. p42.

[78] Martin, ibid. p47.

[79] Stanton, James M. "God Deserves Our Trust" Dallas Morning News, Saturday, July 18, 1998. Copyright ©1998.

[80] From <u>The Concise Columbia Encyclopedia</u>, edited by Paul Lagasse. Copyright ©1995 Columbia University Press. Reprinted with permission of the publisher.

[81] From <u>The Concise Columbia Encyclopedia</u>, edited by Paul Lagasse. Copyright ©1995 Columbia University Press. Reprinted with permission of the publisher.

[82] Wilcox, Lance. "Staging Jonah," <u>Bible Review</u>, February 1995. p.48.

[83] ibid. Wilcox.

[84] Baigent, Michael; Richard Leigh, and Henry Lincoln. <u>Holy Blood, Holy Grail</u>. New York, Delacorte Press. 1982. p16.

[85] Baigent, Ibid. p135.

[86] Spong, Bishop John Shelby, "Rethinking Christianity" Dallas Morning News, Saturday, July 18, 1998. Copyright ©1998.

[87] McDowell, Josh. From <u>More Than A Carpenter</u>. Used by

permission of Tyndale House Publishers, Inc. © 1977. All rights reserved.

[88] McDowell, ibid.

[89] McDowell, Josh. Evidence that Demands a Verdict: Revised Edition. San Bernardino California, Here's Life Publishers. 1979.

[90] McDowell, ibid.

[91] McDowell, ibid.

[92] McDowell, ibid.

[93] Introduction to A Course In Miracles Internet Site: http://nen.sedona.net/circleofa/acimntro.html "What is A Course In Miracles?" No copyright posted. 1999.

[94] The Course Internet site: http://www.hasanadesigns.com/course/course.html "A Course In Miracles" No copyright posted. 1999 .

[95] ACIM: What It Says (Expanded) Internet site: http://www.pix.za/mbs/spirit/acimlong.htm "What It Says" By Robert Perry. No copyright posted. 1999.

[96] Shucman, Helen, Dr. A Course In Miracles: Volume Three Manual For Teachers. Farmingdale, New York, Foundation For Inner Peace. ©1975. p3.

[97] Shucman, ibid. p16.

[98] Shucman, ibid. p32.

[99] Shucman, ibid. p57.

[100] Shucman, ibid. p55.

[101] Redfield, James. The Celestine Vision. New York, Warner Books, Inc. ©1997. p xviii.

[102] Redfield, ibid. p11.

[103] Redfield, ibid. p196.

[104] Redfield, ibid. p26.

[105] Redfield, ibid. p93.

[106] Levi. The Aquarian Gospel of Jesus the Christ. Los Angeles, California, DeVorss & Co., Publishing. ©1964. p254.

[107] Levi, ibid. p255.

[108] Levi, ibid. p13.

[109] Levi, ibid. p14.

[110] Levi, ibid. p119.

[111] <u>The Lost Books of the Bible</u>. New York, Bell Publishing Company. ©1979.

[112] Cranston, Sylvia. <u>HPB; The Extraordinary Life and Influence of Helena Blavatsky, Founder of the Modern Theosophical Movement</u>. New York, G.P. Putnam's Sons. ©1993. p299.

[113] The Theosophical Society Internet site: <u>http://users.aol.com/tstec/hmpage/bio-hpb.htm</u> "H. P. Blavatsky". 1998. No copyright posted.

[114] The Theosophical Society, ibid.

[115] The Theosophical Society Internet site: <u>http://users.aol.com/tstec/hmpage/bio-hso.htm</u> "Henry S. Olcott". 1998. No copyright posted.

[116] From the liner notes of <u>Isis Unveiled</u> by Helena Blavatsky. Quest Books. Used by permission.

[117] The Theosophical Society Internet site: <u>http://users.aol.com/tstec/hmpage/tsideas.htm</u> "Some Basic Concepts of Theosophy," 1998. No copyright posted.

[118] The Theosophical Society, ibid.

[119] The Theosophical Society, ibid.

[120] The Theosophical Society, ibid.

[121] The Theosophical Society, ibid.

[122] The Theosophical Society, ibid.

[123] The Theosophical Society, ibid.

[124] The Theosophical Society, ibid.

[125] Bailey, Alice A. Internet site: <u>http://homepages.ihug.co.nz/~newlight/#WhoIsChrist</u> "New Age Teachings on the Second Coming of Christ". New York, Lucis Publishing. No copyright posted.

[126] Bailey, ibid.

[127] Bailey, ibid.

[128] Bailey, ibid.

[129] Jurriaanse, Aart Internet site: <u>http://inetport.com/~one/ajchrist.html</u> "The Christ: Supreme Head of the Spiritual Hierarchy". 1998. No copyright posted.

[130] Stockbauer, Bette. Internet site: <u>http://inetport.com/~one/bsappoll.html</u> "Apollonius of Tyana." 1998. No copyright posted.

The Millennium Agenda

[131] Stockbauer, ibid.

[132] From <u>The Concise Columbia Encyclopedia</u>, edited by Paul Lagasse. Copyright ©1995 Columbia University Press. Reprinted with permission of the publisher.

[133] From <u>The Concise Columbia Encyclopedia</u>, edited by Paul Lagasse. Copyright ©1995 Columbia University Press. Reprinted with permission of the publisher.

[134] Whiston, William, A.M. translator. <u>The Works of Josephus; Complete and Unabridged</u>. Peabody, Massachusetts, Hendrickson Publishers. 1987.

[135] Jurriaanse, ibid.

[136] Jurriaanse, ibid.

[137] <u>The American Heritage® Dictionary of the English Language, Third Edition</u> copyright © 1992 by Houghton Mifflin Company. Electronic version licensed from InfoSoft International, Inc. All rights reserved.

[138] From <u>The Concise Columbia Encyclopedia</u>, edited by Paul Lagasse. Copyright ©1995 Columbia University Press. Reprinted with permission of the publisher.

[139] Shrine of North America Internet site: <u>http://shrinershq.org/Shrine/affmason.html</u>. July 1998.

[140] Order of the Eastern Star Internet site: <u>http://www.gltexas.org/oestar.htm</u>. July 1998.

[141] Symbolism of The DeMolay Flag Internet Site: <u>http://la-demolay.org/symbolis.htm</u> July 1998.

[142] Symbolism of The DeMolay Flag, ibid.

[143] Marrs, Texe; <u>Circle of Intrigue</u>. Austin Texas, Living Truth Publishers, 1995. p26.

[144] Baigent, Michael; Richard Leigh, and Henry Lincoln. <u>Holy Blood, Holy Grail</u>. New York, Delacorte Press. 1982.

[145] Baigent, ibid. p301.

[146] Baigent, ibid. p302.

[147] Baigent, ibid. p383.

[148] Halbrook, Gary K. "Roman Crucifixion," <u>Biblical Illustrator</u>. Winter 1990. p.2.

[149] Halbrook, ibid. p9.

[150] From <u>The Concise Columbia Encyclopedia</u>, edited by Paul Lagasse. Copyright ©1995 Columbia University Press. Reprinted with permission of the publisher.

[151] Baigent, ibid. p241.

[152] McCabe, Joseph; <u>The Popes and their Church</u>. London, Watts & Co. 1950. p39.

[153] McCabe, ibid. p39.

[154] McCabe, ibid.

[155] McCabe, ibid.

[156] Smith, Uriah; <u>Daniel and the Revelation</u>. Nashville, Tennessee, Southern Publishing Association. ©1944. p119.

[157] Smith, Uriah, ibid. p136.

[158] Smith, Uriah, ibid. p111.

[159] Smith, Louise A. <u>Mary Baker Eddy: Discoverer and Founder of Christian Science</u>. Boston, Massachusetts, The Christian Science Publishing Society. ©1991. p71.

[160] Eddy, Mary Baker. <u>Science and Health with Key to the Scriptures</u>. Boston, Massachusetts, The First Church of Christ, Scientist. p19.

[161] Eddy, ibid. p71.

[162] Eddy, ibid. p70.

[163] Eddy, ibid. p25.

[164] Eddy, ibid. p24.

[165] Eddy, ibid. p11.

[166] Eddy, ibid. p25.

[167] Eddy, ibid.

[168] Eddy, ibid. p30.

[169] Eddy, ibid. p11.

[170] Heindel, Max. <u>The Rosicrucian Cosmo-Conception or Mystic Christianity</u>, ninth edition. Oceanside, California, Rosicrucian Fellowship. Copyright ©1925.

[171] Heindel, ibid. p168.

[172] Heindel, ibid. p168.

[173] Heindel, ibid. p.66.

[174] Heindel, ibid. p147.

[175] Heindel, ibid. p148.

The Millennium Agenda

[176] Heindel, ibid. p.164.

[177] Heindel, ibid. p.164.

[178] Heindel, ibid. p.5.

[179] Heindel, ibid. p.6.

[180] Heindel, ibid. p.287.

[181] Heindel, ibid. p.381.

[182] Heindel, ibid. p.402.

[183] Garraty, John A. <u>The American Nation: A History of the United States to 1877</u>. Third edition. New York, Harper & Row, Publishers. 1975.

[184] Garraty, ibid.

[185] Garraty, ibid.

[186] NaftaNet Internet Site: http://the-tech.mit.edu/Bulletins/ Nafta/01.objective "PART ONE: GENERAL PART: Chapter One: Objectives." 1998. No copyright posted.

[187] World Trade Organization Internet Site: <u>http://www.wto.org/ wto/index.htm</u> . "World Trade Organization." 1998. © 1998 World Trade Organization (WTO). 154 Rue de Lausanne, 1211 Geneva 21, Switzerland.

[188] World Trade Organization, ibid.

[189] World Trade Organization, ibid.

[190] World Trade Organization, ibid.

[191] Cuddy, Dennis L. <u>President Clinton Will Continue the New World Order</u>. Oklahoma City, Oklahoma, Southwest Radio Church. 1993.

[192] Mitchell, Brian, "From Peacekeeper to Babysitter; Is U.S. Defense Strategy Ready For 21st Century?" *Investor's Business Daily*. Wednesday, June 17, 1998. Volume 15, Number 48.

[193] US Treasure Internet Site: http://www.frbatlanta.org/publica/ brochure/fundfac/money.htm#other. December 1998.

Please complete this form to obtain additional copies of this book.

Order Form

E-mail: books@cleffpublishing.com
Phone: (972) 539-7920
Mail: Cleff Publishing
        P.O. Box 270014
        Flower Mound, TX 75027

Visit our internet site at: www.cleffpublishing.com

Please include the following information:

Name: _______________________________________

Address: _____________________________________

City: ____

State: __________________ Postal Code: __________

Telephone (____) ____-________

Please make payment by check or money order.

The Millennium Agenda $12.95
Bulk discounts available.

Shipping:
$3.00 for first book and $2.00 for each additional book.